U.S. Bureau of Indian Affairs

The Cherokee Question

Report of the commissioner of Indian affairs to the president of the United

States, June 15, 1866

U.S. Bureau of Indian Affairs

The Cherokee Question
Report of the commissioner of Indian affairs to the president of the United States, June 15, 1866

ISBN/EAN: 9783337192808

Printed in Europe, USA, Canada, Australia, Japan

Cover: Foto ©Andreas Hilbeck / pixelio.de

More available books at **www.hansebooks.com**

THE CHEROKEE QUESTION.

REPORT

OF THE

COMMISSIONER OF INDIAN AFFAIRS

TO THE

PRESIDENT OF THE UNITED STATES,

JUNE 15, 1866:

BEING

SUPPLEMENTARY TO THE REPORT OF THE COMMISSIONERS APPOINTED
BY THE PRESIDENT TO TREAT WITH THE INDIANS SOUTH
OF KANSAS, AND WHICH ASSEMBLED AT FORT
SMITH, ARK., IN SEPTEMBER, 1865.

WASHINGTON:
GOVERNMENT PRINTING OFFICE.
1866.

THE CHEROKEE QUESTION.

DEPARTMENT OF THE INTERIOR,
OFFICE OF INDIAN AFFAIRS,
Washington, D. C., June 15, 1866.

To ANDREW JOHNSON, *President of the United States:*

The undersigned, Commissioner of Indian Affairs, as president of the southern treaty commission, charged with the duty of negotiating treaties with the several tribes of Indians located in the Indian country or in the State of Kansas, and also with the Indians of the plains west of Kansas and the Indian country, has the honor to submit the following additional report:

All that was done by the commission at Fort Smith, Arkansas, in September last, and how it was done, in discharge of the duty imposed by your order, is already fully reported and published in my annual report for the year 1865, commencing on printed page 296 of that report, to which I beg leave to refer. It will be perceived that the commission was only in part successful, owing, as was asserted by the Indians, and believed by us, to the fact that several of the Indian tribes, including the Cherokees, had not been notified that new treaties with them were desired by the government, and that they had not been properly authorized to make treaties by which any of their lands were to be set apart to the United States, for the use of the friendly tribes in Kansas and elsewhere, as contained in paragraph No. 5, on page No. 299, of the report above referred to, and that the Cherokee national council must first authorize such a treaty to be made, and appoint the commissioners to make it.

No objections were made by the delegation to the several propositions, *except the want of power and authority* in the delegates then present. They promised to return home, and lay these propositions, and all other matters, before their national council, and receive their instructions. No doubt was then expressed that the council would confer all the necessary power upon a commission to make a treaty. They were then informed that the delegation to make a treaty would be called to Washington city, probably, early in December then next, for that purpose. After your commission ascertained that a full treaty, according to our instructions, could not be made, for the above causes, the commission submitted the articles of a partial treaty, as set forth on pages 301 and 302 of the report above referred to, a copy of which was furnished to each tribe. The Cherokees had from the beginning persistently contended that, although it was true that the treaty of October 7, 1861, was made with the Confederate States, that they had done so *under coercion* of the rebel army, and that said treaty was not binding, but as to them was null and void.

On the day the copy of the partial treaty was furnished the Cherokees, September 13, we were informed that John Ross, the principal chief of the Cherokee nation, had arrived in the camp of the Chero-kees. That same evening the several Indian agents were called before the commission, and asked what was the prospect of their several tribes signing the treaty. The Cherokees were first called. Agent Harlan, for the Cherokees, answered that the Cherokees claimed that they had signed the rebel treaty to avoid annihilation by the rebels, and that the same was null and void; that the majority of the nation had all the time been loyal to the United States, and only yielded to power they could not resist; but that as soon as they found a force sufficient to protect them, they joined the Union army and fought to the end of the war, and fought well. And all this he believed, claiming, as they did, that if true, there was no forfeiture on their part. He gave it as his opinion that while the recitals in the preamble remained, asserting a forfeiture of money and lands, they never would sign it; and that he, believing it, would not advise them to do so, unless under a protest that they had signed it to prevent total destruction of their lives and property; but that, under such protest, he would advise them to sign it, and thus save the question of forfeiture for fuller inquiry. He thought they ought to and would sign it under protest.

To this protest the commission consented, and Agent Harlan wrote the protest, which was at once submitted and allowed. You will find this paper on page 304 of the Report of the Commissioner of Indian Affairs, above referred to, as having been made by Colonel Reese at the time of signing the treaty.

Without entering into details in regard to the facts apparent to the commission tending to show that it was the influence of John Ross which, even now, hindered the Cherokee delegates from signing the preliminary treaty, it may be sufficient to say that very shortly after the commission had decided no longer to recognize Ross as chief, under what they deemed ample evidence of his bad influence upon his people, and his steady and sincere disloyalty to the government of the United States, the delegates representing the Cherokee Nation did sign that treaty.

To the commission, when at Fort Smith, it seemed very clear that John Ross, within one month after the late war commenced, clearly took sides with the rebels and against the government of the United States, and that within four months the whole nation, in general mass meeting called by, and after a speech from him, unanimously resolved to throw off their allegiance to the United States, and join the Confederate States. If we were right in our conclusion, (and I still think we were,) John Ross was all the time, and the whole nation after the first four months, disloyal. In August, 1861, General Stand Watie received authority from General McCulloch to raise a battalion in the nation for the rebel service. This force was raised and organized in the December following. In July and August Colonel John Drew, by express authority of Mr. Ross, raised a regiment for the same purpose. General Stand Watie's regiment continued in the rebel service to the end of the war. Colonel Drew's regiment continued in the rebel service until after the battle of Pea Ridge, where most of the regiment fought in the rebel army, and shared in its defeat. Shortly after that memorable defeat, three important events took place : the rebel army was driven out of western Arkansas; the Union army, under Colonel Weir, invaded the Cherokee Nation with a force apparently invincible; and the confederate government was found unable to pay its troops in anything but confederate money—nearly worthless. How much either one or all of these events had to do with Cherokee returning loyalty, others can judge as well as we. The facts exist; the returning loyalty followed closely on the heels of these events. Drew's regiment abandoned the rebel service, and enlisted in the Union army. One other regiment, under Colonel Ritchie, was raised in the Cherokee Nation. Both regiments served the Union to the end of the war.

From August, 1862, until last September, Mr. Ross, all the time chief, had not once been in the Cherokee Nation, and so far as we then knew, or so far as I now know, Mr. Ross had taken no active interest in Cherokee affairs. If his zeal were as great as he now pretends it always has been in the Union cause and for the Cherokee people, whom he had served so long and so successfully, and whose welfare he had so industriously and influentially promoted, it seems somewhat strange to me that he should have abandoned the Union cause in its great peril in 1862, and strange beyond belief that he should for more than three years have abandoned the Cherokee people, when ruin, swift and certain, was overwhelming them; when his influence, acknowledged ability, and foresight were so much needed among his people; and quietly settled himself down in Philadelphia, 1,600 miles from his people, at an expense of some thirty thousand dollars to the nation, while the people whom he loved so well (!) were half starving for want of these thousands so prodigally spent by him.

Inasmuch as the claims of John Ross, and of his party in the Cherokee Nation, to loyalty from the beginning of the war, in April, 1861, are a very important element in the consideration of the subject of the just course to be pursued by the government towards the Cherokees as a people, I beg your indulgence while I devote some space to that particular issue.

In the months of May and June, in 1861, Mr. Ross wrote several letters declaring a firm determination to maintain perfect neutrality. These letters manifest considerable ability and much firmness on the part of Mr. Ross; and yet as early as the 17th day of May he received a letter from Colonel Kenney, commanding the rebel forces at Fort Smith, inquiring what course he, as chief of the Cherokee Nation, intended to pursue in the war then begun. This letter was sent to Mr. Ross by Mr. J. B. Luce, of Fort Smith. I have seen it, but it is now mislaid. This letter was answered by Mr. Ross, and is one of the letters in which Mr. Ross maintains his right to remain neutral. But *to the bearer* of that letter he said verbally, " I claim the right to remain neutral, but if I am ever compelled to take sides, I am a southern man, born in the south, a slaveholder, *and shall take sides with the south* "

On the 12th day of June, 1861, General McCulloch wrote to Mr.

Ross, (see his letter, Appendix, No. 1,) assuring him of his friendship, and determination, if possible, to respect his neutrality on certain conditions, one of which is, that all the Cherokees, so disposed, must be allowed to join the army as home guards, for the purpose of defending themselves in case of invasion from the north; and McCulloch adds: " This, of course, will be in accordance with the views you expressed to me, that in case of an invasion from the north, you would lead your men, yourself, to repel it."

To this, (June 17, 1861,) Mr. Ross answered, (see letter, Appendix, No. 2,) reiterating his firm purpose to remain neutral, and declining to permit the Cherokees to organize as home guards, asserting his friendship for General McCulloch, and for the people of Missouri, Arkansas, and Texas, saying that General McCulloch had mistaken what he had said eight or ten days before, and repeating what he did say, thus: "I informed you that I had taken a neutral position, and would maintain it honestly; but that in case of a foreign invasion, old as I am, I would assist in repelling it. I have not signified any purpose as to an invasion of our soil, and an interference with our rights from the United States or Confederate States, because I have apprehended none, and cannot give my consent to any."

From this correspondence between General McCulloch and Mr. Ross, it is perfectly apparent that there had been a conversation, early in June, between them, entirely different from the written correspondence, in which Mr. Ross had, by his own version, agreed to "assist in repelling foreign invasion," and, in the General's version, said that he would lead his own men to repel an invasion by the north.

There was some reason for this difference. I can see no reason unless it was that a written 'pledge to repel the north might fall, by some accident, into the hands of the northern government and endanger the Cherokee lands and annuities, and that an unwritten pledge would not. Mr. Ross seemed anxious that his public correspondence should show the United States that he refused all overtures from the Confederate States, and that his verbal pledges should fully convince the confederate government that he would be faithful to them and faithless to the United States. In this he succeeded.

Some time previous to the 21st of August, 1861, Mr. Ross gave notice, and called a general mass meeting of the Cherokee Nation, to meet at Tahlequah, to consider Cherokee difficulties. At that meeting several speeches were made, all in favor of repudiating all treaties with the United States, and in favor of a treaty with the Confederate States. Among them was a speech from Chief Ross, afterwards published, but not in my possession. In that speech Mr. Ross stated that the object of the meeting was to consider the propriety of joining the southern confederacy. He gave it as his opinion that it was best for the Cherokees and all other Indians to do so at once; that he was and always had been a southern man—a States' rights man—born in the south, a slaveholder; that the south was fighting for its rights against the oppression of the north; and that the true position of the Indians was with the southern people.

After his speech, the vote (as he says, of the 4,000 Cherokee males then present) was unanimously in favor of abandoning the United States and in favor of joining the confederates. That such was the action of the mass meeting at Tahlequah, such its objects and such its results, is clearly established by his letter to that true patriot Opothleyoholo, the Creek chief, September 19, 1861. (See this letter, Appendix, No. 3.) In this letter Mr. Ross congratulates himself that the "Great Being who overrules all things for good has sustained him in his efforts to unite the hearts and sentiments of the Cherokee people as one man," and that "at a mass meeting of about 4,000 males at Tahlequah we have, with one voice, proclaimed in favor of forming an alliance with the Confederate States, and shall thereby preserve and maintain the brotherhood of the Indian nations in a common destiny." In this letter Mr. Ross acknowledges—rather boasts of—his efforts and success in his work as an emissary among the Cherokees for the benefit of the southern confederacy.

Again, on the 8th day of October, 1861, he wrote to the same Opothleyoholo, acknowledging that he made an address to the mass meeting at Tahlequah, and sent him a copy of it. (See copy of his letter, Appendix, No. 4.) In this letter Mr. Ross says he is grieved to hear so many bad reports, (reports of the defection of Opothleyoholo and his band from the Creek council,) and reiterates his advice to all the red brethren to be united and friendly among themselves.

In June, General Pike and General McCulloch, in company, visited Mr. Ross at Park Hill, his place of residence. For what took place at that meeting, nothing being done at that time in writing, we have the letter of General Pike giving a full and detailed statement, apparently intelligent and candid, of the whole matter in relation to the treaty with the Cherokees and other tribes from first to last, a copy of which letter is annexed. (See Appendix, No. 5.)

The letter of General Pike discloses the fact that Mr. Ross, even at that time, so far as *writing* was concerned, clung to his neutrality, and refused to enter into any treaty with the southern confederacy; but he said that all his interests and feelings were with the south; that General McCulloch informed Mr. Ross that he would respect his neutrality, "and would not invade the Cherokee Nation unless compelled to do so; that General McCulloch kept his word, and that no confederate troops ever were stationed in or marched into the Cherokee country until after the federal troops invaded it," which was *eight months* after the Cherokee treaty had been made with the Confederate States.

This letter effectually disposes of all the pretence of *coercion* from the rebel army, either of Mr. Ross or the Cherokee people. It also shows that what was done they did voluntarily, and that their pretences to the contrary, whether by Mr. Ross or the Cherokee people, were without the smallest particle of truth. This assurance of General McCulloch was given in June, 1861. The treaty was made October 7, 1861, and in June or July, 1862, Colonel Weir, of the Union army, "invaded the Cherokee Nation," after which the rebel army did invade the Cherokee country.

The idea of the plea of coercion was invented when such a plea was wanted to cover up their treachery; but no such plea was ever hinted at until Colonel Weir had invaded the nation. Up to that time Mr. Ross remained unmolested by the confederates, well pleased with their situation, and with the "best treaty we have ever had."

On the 7th page of General Pike's letter he says: "At the request of Mr. Ross I wrote the Cherokee declaration of independence." This declaration of independence and war, the vilest and most vituperative document in print, was adopted by the council and approved by Chief Ross, at the time the council advised and ratified the treaty with the Confederate States. (For that declaration see Appendix, No. 6.)

At the time the treaty was signed and ratified, and this declaration was adopted, General Pike says his party consisted of only five persons, all the white confederates in the nation, and eight or nine companies of Drew's regiment, the friends of Ross and the council, were all who were present at the treaty ground or at its ratification—rather a poor show for *coercion*. Throughout the whole proceedings all seemed to be done freely and cheerfully, like persons doing what they wished to do.

On the same page 7 of General Pike's letter, he says : "Even in May, he (Ross) said to General McCulloch and myself, that if northern troops invaded the Cherokee country, he would head the Cherokees and drive them back ; 'I have borne arms,' he said, 'and though I am old, I can do it again.' " This extract fully proves the truth of the statement of J. B. Luce and General McCulloch, and disposes of the version given by Mr. Ross. Other parts of this letter I will mention hereafter.

On the 19th day of December, 1861, Mr. Ross made a speech to Drew's regiment, at Fort Gibson, in which he said that the treaty was made with the confederacy, to the entire satisfaction of all concerned in it. He used the following language : "It is the very best treaty we have ever made in many particulars, as it secures to us many advantages we have long sought. On the very day the treaty was signed, it was submitted to the national council, then in session, and was there read and deliberated on article by article, and unanimously adopted and confirmed by both houses, and it thus became a law." (See copy of the speech referred to, Appendix, No. 7.)

I refer to this speech to show that Mr. Ross was still urging the Cherokees to adhere to their treaty with the confederacy. The "strange occurrence" which he refers to was the defection of a part of Drew's regiment from the confederate army, and their fighting on the Union side with Opothleyoholo, at Bird's creek, which act he so much deplores ; but tells them they "must" return to duty in the confederate service, and that it is their interest to do so.

January 1, 1862, Mr. Ross wrote to General Pike, acknowledging the receipt of amendments made by the rebel senate to the Cherokee treaty, and informing General Pike that the special session of the Cherokee council was called on the Monday following, for their consideration. (See letters, Appendix, No. 8.)

February 25, 1862, Mr. Ross wrote to General Pike that the amendments to the Cherokee treaty had been ratified, and informing the General that Drew's regiment, according to orders received, had promptly marched toward Fayetteville; says he accompanied them twelve miles; assures the General that the regiment will do its duty whenever the conflict with the *common enemy* shall take place; says he intended to accompany the troops to headquarters to render every aid in his power to repel the *enemy;* and says the mass of the Cherokees are all right in sentiment for the support of their alliance with the southern confederacy." (See copy of letter, Appendix, No. 9.)

He, Mr. Ross, did not at that time think that either he or the Cherokee people were loyal to the United States. Drew's and Watie's regiments had gone to the battle then soon to transpire at Pea Ridge, and there was no other rebel force in the nation; if, as he now says, he was only watching for an opportunity to make his escape, and did escape from the nation on the first opportunity which offered, we are not shown, and I cannot see, anything to prevent him from leaving at the time he wrote the letter.

March 22, 1862, Mr. Ross wrote to General Pike, (see copy of letter, No. 10,) requesting that Drew's regiment might be stationed near the place of his (Ross's) residence. In this letter Mr. Ross asserts the exposure of the northern and eastern borders of the Cherokee nation after the battle of Pea Ridge, and asserts that the treasures and records of the nation are wholly unprotected, and that if even a few lawless men should combine for plunder or mischief, he would be in danger.

If, as he asserts, he was forced by the rebel army to sign the treaty, if he was all the time loyal, if he was only waiting for an opportunity to escape from the rebels to the Union lines, I think this would have been the right time to try it. When, as he asserts in this letter, there was so little rebel force in the nation that it could not keep *out* a few individuals seeking plunder or mischief, I hardly suppose it could keep *in* a man with many relations and friends, and an armed regiment of his own raising, who wished to go out of the nation.

March 24, 1862, Ross to ———. (See Appendix, letter No. 11.) This letter of Mr. Ross is no otherwise important than as it shows the persevering zeal of the writer in the rebel cause.

April 10, 1862, Mr. Ross writes to General Pike, (See copy of letter, Appendix, No. 12.) In this letter he thanks General Pike for stationing Colonel Drew's regiment near Park Hill. He says great anxiety exists, in view of the unprotected condition of the Cherokee country since the battle of Pea Ridge and the withdrawal of General Price's army, and also lest marauding parties of United States soldiers will overrun the country. This letter again shows how easily Mr. Ross might have escaped to the Union lines if he had desired it, when no rebel force but his own friends of Drew's regiment was in the nation, the officers of which, it is claimed, were true Union men appointed by himself.

I will now recur to the letter of General Pike, so often referred to above. On page 4 of that letter General Pike says:

"Meanwhile he (Mr. Ross) had persuaded Opothleyoholo, the Creek leader, not to join the southern States, and had sent delegates to meet the northern and other Indians in council near the Antelope Hills, when they all agreed to be neutral. The object was to take advantage of the war between the States and form a great independent Indian confederation"—and that he saw the letter of Mr. Ross and published it in Texas. This letter I never saw and cannot produce, but I fully believe the statement of General Pike. If this statement is true, and I believe it is, what a commentary it is on the pretended loyalty of Mr. Ross! To pretend and publish that he was loyal to the United States at that time, to draw it mildly, is pitiable effrontery.

Again, General Pike says, same letter, page 10 of original:

"In May, 1862, Lieutenant Colonel William P. Ross visited my camp at Fort McCulloch, near Red river, and said to me that 'the chief would be gratified if he were to receive the appointment of brigadier general in the confederate service.'" This, it will be recollected, was in May, 1862, when there was not, by Mr. Ross's own showing, a confederate soldier, except Drew's regiment, in the Cherokee Nation.

Again, in the same letter, page 11 of the original, General Pike says:

"When Colonel Weir invaded the Cherokee country, Mr. Ross refused to have an interview with him, declaring that the Cherokees would remain faithful to their engagements with the Confederate States. There was not then a confederate soldier in the Cherokee Nation to overawe Mr. Ross or Major Pegg, or any other loyal Cherokee. Mr. Ross sent me a copy of his letter to Colonel Weir, and I had it printed and sent over Texas, to show the people there that the Cherokee chief was loyal to the Confederate States." (See letter of T. J. Mackey, Appendix, No. 13.)

It must be borne in mind that Colonel Weir invaded the Cherokee country the latter part of June, 1862. This refusal was after that date. Mr. Ross at that time had not ascertained that he and the Cherokee Nation had been *coerced* in the preceding August. But a few days afterwards he saw it clearly. He first found it out when Drew's regiment abandoned the confederate service and enlisted in the Union army, as graphically described by General Pike in his letter on page 10:

"It was not customary with the confederate war department to exhibit any great wisdom, and in respect to the Indian country its conduct was disgraceful. Unpaid, unclothed, uncared for, unthanked even, services unrecognized, it was natural the Cherokees should abandon the confederate flag."

This last extract is the key to the loyalty of Mr. Ross and the Cherokee Nation. From the beginning of the war to the invasion by Colonel Weir of the nation, as far as I have been able to learn, not one loyal word had ever been written or spoken by any Cherokee, or by Mr. Ross; nor had one word of complaint ever been made by either of any coercion, although there was nothing to prevent such a complaint being made to the United States government at any time, if such had been the fact. After the soldiers had been in the rebel service ten months, and remaining "unpaid, unclothed, uncared for, unthanked even, services unrecognized," they were easily convinced that they were loyal, and by a slight strain on a lively imagination they could see that they had been loyal to the United States from the first, and that they had been *coerced* into the rebel service, although nobody else even knew that any rebel soldier ever invaded their country or threatened it: but, on the contrary, General McCulloch had promised them (and kept his promise,) that they should not be invaded by the rebels unless to repel the United States army from their country.

As soon as Drew's regiment found they would not be paid, clothed, or thanked, and that they had been loyal from the beginning, and that they had somehow been forced into the rebel army, the regiment *en masse* enlisted in the United States army and abandoned the rebel army. When Mr. Ross found himself abandoned by Drew's regiment, he also found that he had been always loyal, and some excuse was necessary from him. None presented itself more potent than coercion. Colonel Weir sent a regiment after him and brought Mr. Ross to his headquarters. Since then he has professed loyalty to the United States government from the beginning, and claims that he only made the treaty with the Confederate States because he was forced—that he was forced to remain in the nation by the rebel army. And that as soon as he was emancipated by Colonel Weir, he flew to the Union lines, where his heart always was ! With how much truth, or semblance of truth, he makes the claim, in these pages I have attempted to show, from his writings, speeches, conversations, documents, acts. conduct, and the letters of other persons who had the means to know, and did know, the matters about which they wrote and spoke.

I do not know how these things may affect others, but to my mind they are conclusive that Mr. Ross, during the short time in which he kept up the pretence of neutrality in his letters, was, in his private conversations, giving assurances to the rebel leaders that he was a secessionist. and was in fact a secessionist. After the Union defeat at Wilson's creek, when General Lyon lost his life, Mr. Ross thought the Union forever dissolved, and secession an accomplished fact. He then made haste to join the rebellion, and continued faithful until Drew's regiment abandoned him and Colonel Weir took him prisoner, or, as he says, escorted him out of the nation. This appears from his message to the national council, October 9, 1861, when the treaty was ratified. (See that paper, Appendix, A.) Mr. Ross, in that special message to the general council of the Cherokee Nation, uses this language: "Neutrality was proper and wise so long as there remained a reasonable probability that the difficulty between the two sections of the Union would be settled," &c.; "but when there was no longer reason to believe that the union of the States would be continued, there was no cause to hesitate as to the course the Cherokee Nation should pursue." "Our geographical position and domestic institutions allied us to the south." This message gives no proof of having been written by a man under coercion, but the spirit with which it is written shows that the heart and soul of the writer entered into the subject.

That he was ever loyal to the United States I do not believe. His neutral position, which in his letters he maintained for about two months, was only just not disloyal, if taken and maintained in good faith. But even of that excuse his often-repeated verbal declarations, only one month after the war commenced, and while in his letters he was pretending neutrality, entirely deprive him. They show that he was assuring the leading rebels that he was *not* neutral, but actually acting as an active emissary of the confederacy. Now it is perfectly apparent that he was acting with duplicity, and intended to deceive one or the other party, or both. In this he succeeded. This was before the battle of Pea Ridge. After that battle, both Mr. Ross and the Cherokee people thought and said and acted as interest, not loyalty to the United States, dictated. For ten months they had kept two regiments in the field in the confederate service; so far they kept faith with the Confederate States. When Drew's regiment found they were not paid, clothed, or cared for, they abandoned the confederate and joined the Union army, because it was their interest to do so, not because of their loyalty. They had fought for the rebels at Pea Ridge. If they had been paid, clothed, and cared for, it is almost certain we never should have heard their clamor of loyalty or coercion.

Mr. Ross says himself that he raised Drew's regiment for the rebel army before the treaty, and while a Cherokee treaty was in full force with the United States. From that time to the invasion of the Cherokee Nation by the forces under Colonel Weir, every letter, every word, every act of his, so far as we know or have ever heard, or that he has been able to produce, shows that he was actively and zealously at work promoting the success of the rebellion. His activity and zeal seem to have met the approval of the confederate authorities. He seems to have deserved it from them. The Cherokees, two regiments strong, had fought in the battle of Pea Ridge. He says he would have been at headquarters, rendering all the assistance in his power against the common enemy, but for some bad conduct of Watie's men. When he made that lucky escape from the thraldom of the rebel army, and got to the Union lines, all his zeal and activity seemed to have forsaken him. He left the nation, and did not return to it for three years, and, so far as I know, manifested no zeal or activity either in the Union cause he loved so well, or for the Cherokees, who so much needed his counsel, advice, and assistance. There has not been one fact brought to my notice, or of which I have heard, which, to my mind, has the slightest tendency to prove coercion by the rebel army, any threat, or anything to cause even the most timid to think there was any fear of it. If there was, why did he not inform the government of the United States of it? When he thought there was danger of invasion by the Union army he promptly informed the rebel government of it.

The commission at Fort Smith, in September last, seeing what they did of his bad influence upon the Cherokees, and hearing and believing what we heard, that he was opposed to the treaty being signed: and hearing that he was tampering with the Creeks, and believing it, and being satisfied that he had been from the first a secessionist, and believing he still was; being satisfied that he had acted with duplicity, in bad faith, and treacherously towards the government of the United States, and believing that he would continue so to act; being satisfied that he was opposed to entering into any treaty with the United States, and believing that he would continue opposed, although so desirable both to the Cherokee people and the government of the United States for their mutual peace and quiet, and so necessary for the best interest of the Cherokee people—the commission, I repeat, unanimously decided not to recognize John Ross as principal chief of the Cherokee Nation. In that decision I concurred. I was then, and I am still, satisfied that that decision was necessary, right, and proper, and should be adhered to by the government.

For more than thirty years there have been two parties in the Cherokee Nation, known to the country as the Ross and Ridge parties. As the parties still, to some extent, remain the same, I may, in this report, continue so to distinguish them, though Ridge was assassinated by the Ross party in 1839. The formation of these parties was caused, as is believed, by discussions which led to and finally culminated in the treaty of 1835 between the United States and the Cherokee Nation. The Ridge party prevailed and made that treaty. The Ross party opposed it. After the removal of the Cherokees, under that treaty, to their present homes on the Arkansas, the dissatisfaction increased in bitterness, and became a deadly feud. This feud, with greater or less bitterness, still continued, sometimes irritated and sometimes partially modified by other questions, real or imaginary causes, but never forgiven. Early in the late war, after the treaty made with the rebels, the Ridge party raised a regiment, commanded by General Watie, and joined the rebel army, went south, where they and their families generally remain, and continued in that service to the end of the war. A little earlier in 1861 Colonel Drew, under direction of Mr. Ross, raised a regiment in the Ross party, who also joined the rebel army, and continued in that service about ten months, when they deserted the rebel army and immediately joined the Union army, and continued to the end of the war. About the same time, from the Ross party was raised another regiment, (making two regiments of the Ross party in the Union army,) which also remained in the United States service to the end of the war. In June or July, when these two regiments were raised for the Union army. Watie's regiment, with the rebel army, was on the southwest bank of the Arkansas river, where they generally remained for about two years. In July and August, 1862, the Union army, under Colonel Doubleday, and afterwards Colonel Weir, drove the Ridge party, under Stand Watie, from the Cherokee Nation in confusion, capturing all their train and provisions. They abandoned their homes and property to the Ross party, who remained in possession of the nation. For two years marauding parties of the rebel army, composed largely of Cherokees of the Ridge party, crossed the Arkansas river into the Cherokee country and plundered the Ross party until the latter were in as destitute a condition as the former. The depredations were reciprocal, and the black flag seemed to be the banner under which both parties fought. Under these circumstances, the old feud (which never died, but only slept or pretended to sleep short naps, was, of course, revived, and was, I suppose, from the evidence before me, intensified.

Separate delegations from each party are now in this city, called here for the purpose of making a treaty with the United States. They seem wholly unable to agree on any one material proposition.

The Ridge party requires the Cherokee Nation for the present to be divided into two bands, each to make its own laws and execute them, but to remain component parts of the Cherokee Nation, and when (if ever) a reconciliation takes place, to reunite by their own agreement, or be united by the government. That for the present the territory should be divided, so that the two parties shall each enjoy its own without molestation from the other. They consent to sell or set apart to the United States, for the purpose of settling on it the friendly Indians of Kansas, all the Cherokee lands lying west of 95° 30' west longitude, and to sell to the United States the neutral land lying in Kansas for a sum not less than $500,000, with a liberal grant to the several proposed railroads running through the Cherokee country. This is the substance of their propositions.

The Ross party wholly refuse any division for any purpose, and require all who wish to form a part of the Cherokee Nation to come back in a limited time. They agree, like the Ridge party, to sell the neutral land in Kansas, but refuse to sell or set apart any of their lands lying east of the line of 97° west longitude, but they do agree that any of the friendly Indians who will become a part of the Cherokee Nation may settle on and occupy a part of their territory. They will make no grant to railroads, except the right of way over two hundred feet in width to each road, and require the north and south road to pass through Fort Gibson. They offer many other objectionable propositions, not ultimata; but the above are such.

Under the instructions given to the commissioners at Fort Smith for our guidance there, which are still in force for my guidance here. I was compelled to refuse these propositions of the Ross party as wholly inadmissible. They would confirm to the Cherokee people about 6,500,000 acres of land, making about 382 acres each to every man, woman, and child in the Cherokee Nation—an amount ten times larger than is convenient under their present circumstances, and twenty times greater than will be advantageous or convenient when (if ever) they become perfectly civilized. To suffer this amount to lie useless in the hands of the Indians, who cannot use it, and really do not require it, and withhold it from civilization, which does require it, and can and will use it, is to my mind neither wise statesmanship nor good policy.

After several propositions had been made on both sides, and many meetings and conversations had with the Ross party, under my instructions 1 presented them with the substance of what the treaty must contain, set forth in the following paper. (See paper, Appendix, B.)

The reservation therein referred to, east of 95° 30' west longitude, will amount to about one hundred and seventy-seven (177) acres to each Cherokee and freed person, men, women, and children included. This proposition they peremptorily refused. The account of what took place at this meeting was taken down at the time by a stenographer present for that purpose, and is believed to be correct. (See paper in Appendix, marked C.)

1 think the offer of 320 acres to the Ross party much larger than their necessities demand. It is proposed to give them that portion of the country where they are now residing, so that they will not be disturbed in their homes or property by the contemplated division.

It will be seen from the foregoing that the feeling existing between the Ross and Ridge parties is extremely bitter, and all attempts at reconciliation have heretofore proved unavailing. It was to meet this state of things that in the original instructions by the President to the commission about to start for Fort Smith last fall the following paragraph was inserted:

"Strife and dissension may, in some instances, have prevailed to such extent in a particular nation or tribe as to result in the formation of contending parties. If it is impracticable to reconcile them to each other and re-establish their former harmonious relations as members of the same organization, you may recognize them as distinct communities. In that event you will authorize a division, on equitable terms, of its funds and annuities, and the settlement of each party on separate portions of their reservation, to be clearly marked by metes and bounds. Such parties will thereafter be treated as independent tribes. You will, however, assure them of the anxious desire of the President that all past differences should be buried in oblivion, and that they should live together as brothers. Your consent to the arrangement above suggested will not be given until all efforts to restore harmony and union shall have proved utterly unavailing."

During the conferences at Fort Smith, at my suggestion a committee of five from each party met for the purpose of compromising and settling their differences, but was unable to accomplish any good result, the Ross party neither at Fort Smith or here having shown any disposition to adjust their differences with the Ridge party upon a basis of justice and equity.

After having made earnest and repeated efforts to harmonize these difficulties, and finding all such efforts fruitless, it has been apparent that the only course left for the commissioners under the above-cited instructions was to provide for a just and equitable division of the lands and funds of the Cherokee people, and to treat the two parties as "distinct communities." Those instructions must govern the action of this office, unless modified or withdrawn. They have not been modified or withdrawn.

Since the Cherokees have been in this city the Ross party have issued three pamphlets, copies of which accompany this report, marked D, E. and F.

The first one issued (D) is but a general history of the Cherokee difficulties, dangers and trials, and an attempt to prove that the Cherokees were loyal to the United States, and *coerced* into the rebellion. Upon this question I have given my views in these pages.

The second pamphlet (E) is mostly a defence of John Ross, strongly insisting on his loyalty, zeal, and ability in the Union cause. On his loyalty I have said all I wish to say, except this: that at Fort Smith, when the paper refusing any longer to recognize him as the principal chief of the Cherokee Nation was under consideration, he asked the privilege of replying *instanter*, which was readily granted. He then spoke nearly an hour, and showed his loyalty by proving his neutrality to the last of June: said he had always been loyal and then was, and then stopped. Leave was granted his nephew, William P. Ross, to take time to prepare himself and reply for him. W. P. Ross, at the time appointed, appeared, and made a very creditable speech in favor of his uncle, John Ross; read a great number of letters asserting his neutrality, and proving it up to the last of June, 1861, about two months after the rebellion commenced; and then *he* stopped. Pamphlet E, under consideration, prepared under Mr. Ross's eye in this city, asserts his loyalty, as his own speech and the speech of W. P. Ross had done before, and refers to the same letters and papers referred to before by himself and W. P. Ross. I therefore am forced to the conclusion that all that can be said for his loyalty has been said; and all the evidence of loyalty is, that for two months he asserted his neutrality, and that in the first half of that time he had given General Pike and McCulloch full assurance that he would, in a short time, betray the United States and join the rebellion, and did do it.

The pamphlet marked F is but a document arguing the reasonableness of their offer, and the unreasonableness of my demand in the paper marked B in the Appendix. I have already said what I had to say about the negotiation, unconscious that I have departed in any way from my instructions.

The Ridge party has published two pamphlets in answer to those published by the Ross party. Whatever else may be said of all these pamphlets, I do not think any one can say that there is any want of cayenne to season them. They all show a keen hostility, the one party against the other, and that neither has yet forgotten its ancient grudge. or forgiven it. (See pamphlets marked G and H.)

In the paper heretofore referred to. marked B, I have insisted on a separation, into two bands, of the Cherokees. I have for another purpose, in this report, mentioned the ancient feud of the Cherokees. That feud still exists, as is shown by the pamphlets above set forth: and that it has always existed since it first arose there can be no doubt. At different periods of Cherokee history it has shown itself. Nearly every distinguished man of the Ridge party has been killed, and Ridge himself, twenty-eight years ago. fell by the assassin's knife, while many of lesser note on both sides. growing out of this

Ross and Ridge feud, have died by violence. The Ridge party joined the rebellion, and with their families went south, where they mostly now are. The Ross party say they will forgive them, reinstate them in their homes, and afford them protection to life, liberty, and property, but they must come back and submit to their jurisdiction. The Ridge party say their offence is against the United States, and not against the Cherokee Nation, which has no right to talk of forgiveness; they can have no confidence in these promises of the Ross party, or any other they may make; they say they have trusted them before, and been deceived. That they are afraid of assassination and depredations on their liberty and property, but more afraid of judicial murders, robberies, and deprivations of liberty, than from open assault; and say they never can and never will try to live with the Ross party until there is a decided change, of which they say they can as yet see no signs.

Which party is right, or nearest right, or which is wrong or most wrong, I have no means of determining. That there is great ill-feeling is agreed by both parties; but they do not agree us to the extent of the hatred. Being myself in doubt, I applied to those who had been longest in the neighborhood, or had lived among them, and such as would be most likely to have a correct opinion as to the probability of the two parties harmonizing and living together in peace and security. I have directed letters to the following named gentlemen, and received their several answers, which will be found in the Appendix hereto:

Answer from Judge Harlan, Cherokee agent, marked I; answer from Judge Tebbetts, marked J; an answer from Charles H. Johnson, marked K; answer from R. T. Van Horn, member of Congress from Missouri, marked L; answer from General Blunt, marked M; answer from General D. H. Cooper, marked N; answer from J. B. Luce, marked O.

These are all the answers that I have received to my letter of inquiry; but these are enough. Every one of these gentlemen is well acquainted with the feuds in the Cherokee Nation; some of them from the time they removed from Georgia to the Arkansas river. All speak of those feuds as of the most deadly kind, and each and all express the opinion that the two parties never can live together in peace, and that they had better be separated for the quiet of the country. I have not yet found one person who dissented from this opinion, except the members of the Ross delegation; and against that opinion that they can live together, I would offset the opinion of the Ridge delegation, equally or even more positive, that they cannot. I entertain no doubt but that it is the duty of the United States to insist upon their separation for the peace of the country, and for the welfare of the Indians themselves.

From the various considerations adduced, and documents referred to in this report, the following conclusions are obtained, viz:

That after protracted and diligent efforts, continuing about five months, to make some satisfactory arrangements with the delegates

2

representing the Cherokee national authorities, by which the government of the United States could expect to fulfil its guarantee to protect the nation from domestic strife, such efforts failed.

That there is no reasonable probability of the two parties being able to harmonize their difficulties and live together in peace.

That under the original instructions furnished by the Executive to the commissioners, there remained but one course to pursue, to wit, to make the best possible arrangements for the division of the people and partition of the national property and funds.

That, by manifold proofs, the Ross party, which refuses to take part in these necessary arrangements, has been so far identified with the late rebellion that they cannot, in common justice and fairness, appeal to loyal hearts in the government of the United States to take their part, to the exclusion of the rights of other parties of the same nation, who, like the Ross party, entered into close relations with the leaders of that rebellion.

Acting under special instructions from the Secretary of the Interior, who has been familiar with the whole course of the negotiation, "to settle and pay the necessary expenses incurred by the delegates representing the northern Cherokees in coming to this city and during their sojourn, and to advance enough to defray their expenses home, and to carry into effect the oral and written instructions of the President in relation to the southern Cherokees," I have, with Commissioners Sells and Parker, concluded and signed, on the 13th instant, articles of agreement with the delegates of the southern Cherokees, providing for their separate existence and the division of the national property. This document is laid before you for your constitutional action. If it shall meet with your approval, and be ratified, and go into full effect, we may reasonably hope for a cessation of the long-continued troubles of the Cherokee people.

Very respectfully, your obedient servant,

D. N. COOLEY, *Commissioner.*

APPENDIX.

No. 1.

General McCulloch to John Ross.

HEADQUARTERS McCULLOCH'S BRIGADE,
Fort Smith, Ark., June 12, 1861.

SIR: Having been sent by my government (the Confederate States of America) to take command of the district embracing the Indian territory, and to guard it from invasion by the people of the north, I take the first opportunity of assuring you of the friendship of my government, and the desire that the Cherokees and other tribes in the territory unite their fortunes with the confederacy. I hope that you, as chief of the Cherokees, will meet me with the same feelings of friendship that actuate me in coming among you, and that I may have your hearty co-operation in our common cause against a people who are endeavoring to deprive us of our rights. It is not my desire to give offence or interfere with any of your rights or wishes, and shall not do so unless circumstances compel me. The neutral position you wish to maintain will not be violated without good cause. In the mean time those of your people who are in favor of joining the confederacy must be allowed to organize into military companies as home guards for the purpose of defending themselves in case of invasion from the north. This, of course, will be in accordance with the views you expressed to me, that, in case of an invasion from the north, you would lead your men yourself to repel it.

Should a body of men march into your territory from the north, or if I have an intimation that a body is in line of march for the territory from that quarter, I must assure you that I will at once advance into your country if I deem it advisable.

I have the honor to be, sir, your obedient servant,

BEN. McCULLOCH.
Brigadier General, Commanding.

His Excellency JOHN ROSS,
Chief of the Cherokee Nation.

No. 2.

John Ross's reply to the above.

EXECUTIVE DEPARTMENT,
Park Hill, C. N., June 17, 1861.

SIR: I have the honor to acknowledge by the first return mail the receipt of your communication, dated at Fort Smith, Ark., the 12th instant, informing me that you have been sent by the government of the Confederate States of America to take command of the district embracing the Indian territory, and to guard it from invasion by the people of the north. For the expression of your friendship, be pleased to accept my heartfelt thanks, and the assurance that I cherish none other than a similar sentiment for yourself and people; am also gratified to be informed that you will not interfere with any of our rights and wishes, unless circumstances compel you to do so, nor violate or molest our neutrality without good cause. In regard to the pending conflict between the United States and the Confederate States, I have already signified my purpose to take no part in it whatever, and have admonished the Cherokee people to pursue the same course. The determination to adopt that course was the result of considerations of law and policy; and seeing no reasons to doubt its propriety, I shall adhere to it in good faith, and hope that the Cherokee people will not fail to follow my example. I have not been able to see any reason why the Cherokee Nation should take any other course, for it seems to me to be dictated by their treaties, and sanctioned by wisdom and humanity; it ought not to give ground for complaint to either side, and should cause our rights to be respected by both. Our country and institutions are our own. However small the one or humble the other, they are as sacred and valuable to us as are those of your own populous and wealthy State to yourself and your people. We have done nothing to bring about the conflict in which you are engaged with your own people, and I am unwilling that my people shall become its victims. I am determined to do no act that shall furnish any pretext to either of the contending parties to overrun our country and destroy our rights. If we are destined to be overwhelmed, it shall not be through any agency of mine. The United States are pledged not to disturb us in our rights, nor can we for a moment suppose that your government will do it, as the avowed principles upon which it is struggling for an acknowledged existence are the rights of the States and freedom from outside interference. The Cherokee people and government have given every assurance in their power of their sympathy and friendship for the people of Arkansas and of other Confederate States, unless it be in voluntarily assuming an attitude of hostility towards the government of the United States, with whom their treaties exist, and from whom they are not experiencing any new burdens or exactions. That I cannot advise them to do, and hope that their good faith in adhering to the requirements of their treaties, and of their friendship for all the whites, will be manifested by strict observance of the neutrality enjoined. Your demand, that those people of the nation who are in favor of joining the confederacy be allowed to organize into military companies as home guards for the purpose of defending themselves in case of invasion from the north, is most respectfully declined. I cannot give my consent to any such organization, for very obvious reasons: 1st. it would be a palpable violation of my position as a neutral; 2d, it will place in our midst organized companies not authorized by our laws, but in violation of treaty, and who would soon become efficient instruments in stirring up domestic strife, and creating internal difficulties among the Cherokee people. As in this connexion you have misapprehended a remark made in conversation at our interview some eight or ten days ago, I hope you will allow me to repeat what I did say: I informed you that I had taken a neutral position, and would maintain it honestly; but that in case of a foreign invasion, old as I am, I would assist in repelling it. I have not signified any purpose as to an invasion of our soil and an interference with our rights from the United or Confederate States, because I have apprehended none, and cannot give my consent to any.

I have the honor to be, sir, your obedient servant,
JOHN ROSS,
Principal Chief Cherokee Nation.

Brig. Gen. BEN. McCULLOCH,
Com'g Troops of Confederate States, Fort Smith, Ark.

No. 3.

John Ross's letter to Opothleyoholo, Creek chief, September, 1861.

PARK HILL, CHEROKEE NATION, *September 19, 1861.*

FRIENDS AND BROTHERS: I have received a few lines from you, written on the back of a hasty note which I had written to the chiefs and headmen of your nation, and from which the following is an extract:

"BROTHERS: I am gratified to inform you that the Great Being who overrules all things for good has sustained me in my efforts to unite the hearts and sentiments of the Cherokee people as one man; and at a mass meeting of about four thousand males, at Tahlequah, with one voice we have proclaimed in favor of forming an alliance with the Confederate States, and shall thereby preserve and maintain the brotherhood of the Indian nations in a common destiny."

Brothers, if it is your wish to know whether I had written the above note or not, I will tell you that I did; and in order that you may be fully informed of the whole proceedings of the Cherokee people at the mass meeting stated, and of the reasons which influenced the people to adopt them, I send you herewith several printed copies of my address to the people in convention, and of the resolutions adopted by them on that occasion. I wish you to have them carefully read and correctly interpreted, in order that you may fully understand them.

Brothers, my advice and desire, under the present extraordinary crisis, is for all the red brethren to be united among themselves in the support of our common rights and interests by forming an alliance of peace and friendship with the Confederate States of America.

Your friend and brother,
JOHN ROSS,
Principal Chief of the Cherokee Nation.

To OPOTHLEYOHOLO *and others of the*

John Ross to Opothleyoholo, October 8, 1861.

TAHLEQUAH, CHEROKEE NATION, *October* 8, 1861.

FRIENDS AND BROTHERS: Some short time since I received a few lines from you, written on the back of a note of mine to the chiefs and headmen of the Creek nation, informing them that the Cherokee people had resolved in favor of forming an alliance of peace and friendship with the southern confederacy, and you wished to know if I had written that note. I replied that I had; at the same time I sent you a printed copy of my address to a mass meeting of about 4,000 of the Cherokee people; also of their resolutions on that occasion, authorizing a treaty of alliance with the Confederate States. I furthermore informed you that my advice to all the red brethren was to be united and friendly among themselves. I have not heard from you since.

Brothers, I am grieved to hear of so many bad reports which have been circulated throughout the land; many of them are no doubt false and without foundation, and which, if not corrected and silenced, might lead to trouble and bloodshed. They should, by all means, be checked, if possible.

Motey Kennard, as chief of your nation, has appealed to me for the mediation of your Cherokee brethren, for the purpose of reconciling difficulties alleged to exist among your people in consequence of the late treaty entered into with General Pike.

I have promptly consented to do all in my power to restore peace among my brethren; and in order to enable me to act efficiently as a true and faithful brother, I have obtained from General Pike letters of safeguard for the protection of yourself and friends in coming to this place and returning home in safety, under the penalty of death for violating them. I have, therefore, appointed my friend and associate chief, Hon. Jos. Vann, to head a delegation on a mission of peace, and to make you a friendly visit; to hold a free and brotherly talk with you, face to face, that you may fully understand the true position of your Cherokee brethren, and especially to invite you and your personal friends to come and visit your Cherokee brethren now assembled in national council at this place, where we may all smoke the pipe of peace and friendship around our great council fire kindled at Tahlequah eighteen years ago, and that all misunderstanding among the family of our red brethren may forever be buried in oblivion.

Your friend and brother, Hon. Jos. Vann, who is bearer of important papers to you, will explain more fully the objects of his mission.

I sincerely hope that you will not fail to come with him, to shake the hands of brotherly friendship with your Cherokee brethren.

Your friend and brother,

JOHN ROSS,
Principal Chief Cherokee Nation.

To OPOTHLEYOHOLO *and others.*

MEMPHIS, TENNESSEE, *February* 17, 1866.

SIR: I have received, to-day, a copy of the "memorial" of the "Southern Cherokees," to the President, Senate and House of Representatives, in reply to the memorial of other Cherokees, claiming to be "loyal."

It is not for me to take any part in the controversy between the two portions of the Cherokee people, nor have I any interest that could lead me to side with one in preference to the other; nor am I much inclined, having none of the rights of a citizen, to offer to testify in any matter, when my testimony may not be deemed worthy of credit, as that of one not yet restored to respectability and credibility by a pardon.

But, as I know it to be contemptible as well as false for Mr. John Ross and the "loyal" memorialists to pretend that they did not voluntarily engage themselves by treaty stipulations to the Confederate States, and as you have desired my testimony, I have this to say, and I think no man will be bold enough to deny any part of it.

In May, 1861, I was requested by Mr. Toombs, secretary of state of the Confederate States, to visit the Indian country as commissioner, and assure the Indians of the friendship of those States. The convention of the State of Arkansas, anxious to avoid hostilities with the Cherokees, also applied to me to act as such commissioner. I accordingly proceeded to Fort Smith, where some five or six Cherokees called upon General McCulloch and myself, representing those of the Cherokees who sympathized with the south, in order to ascertain whether the Confederate States would protect them against Mr. Ross and the Pin Indians, if they should organize and take up arms for the south. We learned that some attempts to raise a secession flag in the Cherokee country on the Arkansas had been frustrated by the menace of violence; and those who came to meet us represented the Pin organization to be a secret society, established by Evan Jones, a missionary, and at the service of Mr. John Ross, for the purpose of abolitionizing the Cherokees and putting out of the way all who sympathized with the southern States.

The truth was, as I afterwards learned with certainty, the secret organization in question, whose members for a time used as a mark of their membership a *pin* in the front of the hunting-shirt, was really established for the purpose of depriving the half-breeds of all political power, though Mr. Ross, himself a Scotchman, and a Mc-Donald both by the father and the mother, was shrewd enough to use it for his own ends. At any rate, it was organized and in *full* operation long before secession was thought of.

General McCulloch and myself assured those who met us at Fort Smith that they should be protected, and agreed to meet at an early day, then fixed, at Park Hill, where Mr. Ross resided. Upon that I sent a messenger west with letters to five or six prominent members

of the anti-Ross party, inviting them to meet me at the Creek agency
two days after the day on which General McCulloch and I were to
meet at Park Hill.

I did not expect to effect any arrangement with Mr. Ross, and my
intention was to treat with the heads of the southern party—Stand
Watie and others.

When we met Mr. Ross at Park Hill he refused to enter into any
arrangement with the Confederate States. He said that his intention
was to maintain the neutrality of his people; that they were a small
and weak people, and would be ruined and destroyed if they engaged
in the war; and that it would be a cruel thing if we were to engage
them in our quarrel. But he said all his interests and all his feelings were with us, and he knew that his people must share the fate
and fortunes of Arkansas. We told him that the Cherokees could not
be neutral. We used every argument in our power to change his determination, but in vain, and, finally, General McCulloch informed
him that he would respect the neutrality of the Cherokees, and would
not enter their country with troops, or place troops in it, unless it
should become necessary in order to expel a federal force, or to
protect the southern Cherokees.

So we separated. General McCulloch kept his word, and no confederate troops ever were stationed in, or marched into, the Cherokee
country, until after the federal troops invaded it.

Before leaving the nation I addressed Mr. Ross a letter, which I
afterwards printed and circulated among the Cherokee people. In
it I informed him that the Confederate States would remain content
with his pledge of neutrality, although he would find it impossible to
maintain that neutrality; that I should not again offer to treat with
the Cherokees; and that the Confederate States would not consider
themselves bound by my proposition to pay the Cherokees for the
neutral land if they should lose it in consequence of the war. I had
no further communication with Mr. Ross until September. Meanwhile he had persuaded Opothleyoholo, the Creek leader, not to
join the southern States, and had sent delegates to meet the northern and other Indians in council near the Antelope Hills, where they
all agreed to be neutral. The purpose was to take advantage of the
war between the States, and form a great independent Indian confederation. I defeated all that by treating with the Creeks at the
very time that their delegates were at the Antelope Hills in council.

When I had treated with them and with the Choctaws and Chickasaws, at the North Fork of the Canadian, I went to the Seminole
agency and treated with the Seminoles. Thence I went to the Wichita agency, having previously invited the Reserve Indians to return there, and invited the prairie Comanches to meet me. After
treating with these, I returned by Fort Arbuckle, and before reach-
ing there met a nephew of Mr. Ross and a Captain Fields, on
the prairie, bearing a letter to me from Mr. Ross and his council, with
a copy of the resolutions of the council, and an invitation, in pressing
terms, to repair to the Cherokee country and enter into a treaty.

I consented, fixed a day for meeting the Cherokees, and wrote Mr.

Ross to that effect, requesting him also to send messengers to the Osages, Quapaws. Shawnees, Senecas, &c., and invite them to meet me at the same time. He did so, and at the time fixed I went to Park Hill, and there effected treaties.

When I first entered the Indian country, in May, I had as an escort one company of mounted men. I went in advance of them to Park Hill. General McCulloch went there without an escort. At the Creek agency I sent the company back; I then remained without escort or guard until I had made the Seminole treaty; camping with my little party and displaying the confederate flag. When I went to the Wichita country I took an escort of Creeks and Seminoles; these I discharged at Fort Arbuckle, on my return, and went, accompanied by four young men, through the Creek country to Fort Gibson, refusing an escort of Creeks offered me on the way.

From Fort Gibson eight or nine companies of Colonel Drew's regiment of Cherokees, chiefly full-bloods and Pins, escorted me to Park Hill. This regiment was raised by order of the national council, and its officers appointed by John Ross; his nephew, William P. Ross. secretary of the nation, being lieutenant colonel, and Thomas Pegg. president of the national committee, being its major.

I encamped with my little party near the residence of the chief, unprotected even by a guard, and with the confederate flag flying. The terms of the treaty were fully discussed, and the Cherokee authorities dealt with me on equal terms. Mr. John Ross had met me as I was on my way to Park Hill escorted by the national regiment, and had welcomed me to the Cherokee Nation in an earnest and enthusiastic speech, and seemed to me throughout to be acting in perfect good faith. I acted in the same way with him.

After the treaties were signed I presented Colonel Drew's regiment a flag, and the chief in a speech exhorted them to be true to it, and afterwards, at his request, I wrote the Cherokee declaration of independence, which is printed with the memorial of the southern Cherokees. I no more doubted then that Mr. Ross's whole heart was with the south than that mine was. Even in May he said to General McCulloch and myself that if northern troops invaded the Cherokee country, he would head the Cherokees and drive them back. "I have borne arms," he said, "and though I am old I can do it again."

At the time of the treaty there were about nine hundred Cherokees of Colonel Drew's regiment encamped near and fed by me, and Colonel Watie, who had almost abandoned the idea of raising a regiment. had a small body of men, not more, I think, than eighty or ninety, at Tahlequah. When the flag was presented Colonel Watie was present. and after the ceremony the chief shook hands with him and expressed his warm desire for union and harmony in the nation.

The gentlemen whom I had invited to meet me in June at the Creek agency did not do so. They were afraid of being murdered. they said, if they openly sided with the south. In October they censured me for treating with Mr. Ross, and were in an ill humor, saying that the regiment was raised in order to be used to oppress them.

The same day that the Cherokee treaty was signed, the Osages, Quapaws, Shawnees, and Senecas signed treaties, and the next day they had a talk with Mr. Ross at his residence, smoked the great pipe, and renewed their alliance, being urged by him to be true to the Confederate States.

I protest that I believed Mr. John Ross at this time, and for long after, to be as sincerely devoted to the confederacy as I myself was. He was frank, cheerful, earnest, and evidently believed that the independence of the Confederate States was an accomplished fact. I should dishonor him if I believed that he then dreamed of abandoning the confederacy, or turning the arms of the Cherokees against us in case of a reverse.

Before I left the Cherokee country, part of the Creeks under Hopoi-ilthli-Yahola left their homes under arms, and threatened hostilities. Mr. Ross, at my request, invited the old chief to meet him, and urged him to unite with the Confederate States. Colonel Drew's regiment was ordered into the Creek country, and afterwards, on the eve of the action at Bird creek, abandoned Colonel Cooper, rather than fight against their neighbors. But after the action the regiment was again reorganized. The men were eager to fight, they said, against the Yankees, but did not wish to fight their own brethren, the Creeks.

When General Curtis entered northwestern Arkansas in February, 1862, I sent orders from Fort Smith to Colonel Drew to move towards Evansville and receive orders from General McCulloch. Colonel Watie's regiment was already under General McCulloch's command. Colonel Drew's men moved in advance of Colonel Watie with great alacrity, and showed no want of zeal at Pea Ridge.

I do not know that any one was scalped at that place, or in that action, except from information. None of my officers knew it at the time. I heard of it afterwards. I cannot say to which regiment those belonged who did it, but it has been publicly charged on some of the same men who afterwards abandoned the confederate cause, and, enlisting in the federal service, were sent into Arkansas to ravage it.

After the actions at Pea Ridge and Elkhorn, the regiment of Colonel Drew was moved to the mouth of the Illinois, where I was able, after a time, to pay them $25 each, the commutation for six months' clothing, in confederate money. Nothing more, owing to the wretched management of the confederate government, was ever paid them; and the clothing procured for them was plundered by the commands of Generals Price and Van Dorn. The consequence was that when Colonel Weir entered the Cherokee country, the Pin Indians joined him en masse.

I had procured at Richmond, and paid Mr. Lewis Ross, treasurer of the Cherokee Nation, about the 4th of March, 1862, in the chief's house and in the chief's presence, the moneys agreed to be paid them by treaty, being about $70,000 (I think) in coin, and, among other sums, $150,000 in confederate treasury notes loaned the nation by way of advance on the price expected to be paid for the neutral

land. This sum had been promised in the treaty at the earnest solicitation of Mr. John Ross, and it was generally understood that it
was desired for the special purpose of redeeming scrip of the nation
issued long before, and much of which was held by Mr. Ross and his
relatives. That such was the case, I do not know. I only know that
the moneys were paid, and that I have the receipts for them, which,
with others, I shall file in the Indian office.

In May, 1862, Lieut. Colonel William P. Ross visited my camp at
Fort McCulloch, near Red river, and said to me that the "chief"
would be gratified if he were to receive the appointment of brigadier
general in the confederate service. I did not ask him if he was authorized by the chief to say so, but I did ask him if he were sure that
the appointment would gratify him, and being so assured I promised
to urge the appointment. I did so more than once, but never received a reply. It was not customary with the confederate war department to exhibit any great wisdom, and in respect to the Indian
country its conduct was disgraceful. Unpaid, unclothed, uncared
for, unthanked even, and their services unrecognized, it was natural the Cherokees should abandon the confederate flag.

When Colonel Weir invaded the Cherokee country, Mr. Ross refused to have an interview with him, declaring that the Cherokees
would remain faithful to their engagements with the Confederate
States. There was not then a confederate soldier in the Cherokee
Nation to overawe Mr. Ross or Major Pegg, or any other "loyal"
Cherokee. Mr. Ross sent me a copy of his letter to Colonel Weir,
and I had it printed and sent over Texas, to show the people there
that the Cherokee chief was "loyal" to the Confederate States.

Afterwards, when Stand Watie's regiment and the Choctaws were
sent over the Arkansas into the Cherokee country, and Mr. Ross
considered his life in danger from his own people, in consequence of
their ancient feud, he allowed himself to be taken prisoner by the
federal troops. At the time, I believed that if white troops had been
sent to Park Hill, who would have protected him against Watie's men,
he would have remained at home and adhered to the confederacy.
For either he was true to his obligations to the Confederate States,
voluntarily entered into—true at heart and in his inmost soul—or else
he is falser and more treacherous than I can believe him to be.

The simple truth is, Mr. Commissioner, that the "loyal" Cherokees
hated Stand Watie and the half-breeds, and were hated by them. They
were perfectly willing to kill and scalp Yankees; and when they were
hired to change sides, and twenty-two hundred of them were organized into regiments in the federal service, they were just as ready
to kill and scalp when employed against us in Arkansas. We did not
pay and clothe them, and the United States did. They scalped for
those who paid, fed, and clothed them. As to loyalty, they had none
at all.

I entered the Indian country in May, and left it in October. For five
months I travelled and encamped in it, unprotected by white troops,
alone with but four young men, treating with the different tribes. If
there had been any "loyalty" among the Indians, I could not have gone

a mile in safety. Ho-poi-ilth-thli-Yahola was not "loyal." He feared the McIntoshes, who had raised troops, and who he thought meant to kill him for killing their father long years before. He told me that he did not wish to fight against the southern States, but only that the Indians should all act together. If Mr. Ross had treated with us at first, all the Creeks would have done the same. If Stand Watie and his party took one side, John Ross and his party were sure in the end to take the other, especially when that other proved itself the stronger

So far from the Watie party overawing the party which upheld Mr. Ross, I know it to be true that they were afraid to actively co-operate with the Confederate States, to organize, to raise secession flags, or even to meet me and consult with me. They feared that Colonel Drew's regiment would be used to harass them, and they never dreamed of forcing the authorities into a treaty.

After the actions at Elkhorn, murders were continually complained of by Colonels Watie and Drew, and the chief solicited me to place part of Colonel Drew's regiment at or near Park Hill, to protect the government and its records. I did so. There never was a time when the "loyal" Cherokees had not the power to destroy the southern ones.

As to myself, I dealt fairly and openly with all the Indians. I used no threats of force or compulsion with any of them. The "loyal" Cherokees joined us because they believed we should succeed, and left us when they thought we should not. At their request I wrote their declaration of independence and acceptance of the issues of war; and if any men voluntarily, and with their eyes open, and of their own motion, acceded to the secession movement, it was John Ross and the people whom he controlled.

I am, sir, very respectfully, your obedient servant,

ALBERT PIKE.

D. N. COOLEY, Esq., *Commissioner of Indian Affairs.*

No. 6.

Declaration by the people of the Cherokee Nation of the causes which have impelled them to unite their fortunes with those of the Confederate States of America.

When circumstances beyond their control compel one people to sever the ties which have long existed between them and another state or confederacy, and to contract new alliances and establish new relations for the security of their rights and liberties, it is fit that they should publicly declare the reasons by which their action is justified.

The Cherokee people had its origin in the south; its institutions are similar to those of the southern States, and its interests identical with theirs.

Long since it accepted the protection of the United States of

America, contracted with them treaties of alliance and friendship, and allowed themselves to be, to a great extent, governed by their laws.

In peace and in war they have been faithful to their engagements with the United States. With much of hardship and injustice to complain of, they resorted to no other means than solicitation and argument to obtain redress. Loyal and obedient to the laws and the stipulations of their treaties, they served under the flag of the United States, shared the common dangers, and were entitled to a share in the common glory, to gain which their blood was freely shed on the field of battle.

When the dissensions between the southern and northern States culminated in a separation of State after State from the Union, they watched the progress of events with anxiety and consternation. While their institutions and the contiguity of their territory to the States of Arkansas, Texas, and Missouri made the cause of the seceding States necessarily their own cause, their treaties had been made with the United States, and they felt the utmost reluctance even in appearance to violate their engagements, or set at naught the obligations of good faith.

Conscious that they were a people few in numbers compared with either of the contending parties, and that their country might with no considerable force be easily overrun and devastated, and desolation and ruin be the result if they took up arms for either side, their authorities determined that no other course was consistent with the dictates of prudence, or could secure the safety of their people and immunity from the horrors of a war waged by an invading enemy, than a strict neutrality, and in this decision they were sustained by a majority of the nation.

That policy was accordingly adopted and faithfully adhered to.

Early in the month of June of the present year the authorities of the nation declined to enter into negotiation for an alliance with the Confederate States, and protested against the occupation of the Cherokee country by their troops, or any other violation of their neutrality. No act was allowed that could be construed by the United States to be a violation of the faith of treaties.

But Providence rules the destinies of nations, and events, by inexorable necessity, overrule human resolutions. The number of the Confederate States has increased to eleven, and their government is firmly established and consolidated. Maintaining in the field an army of two hundred thousand men, the war became for them but a succession of victories. Disclaiming any intention to invade the northern States, they sought only to repel invaders from their own soil, and to secure the right of governing themselves. They claimed only the privilege, asserted by the declaration of American independence, and on which the right of the northern States themselves to self-government is founded, of altering their form of government when it became no longer tolerable, and establishing new forms, for the security of their liberties.

Throughout the Confederate States we saw this great revolution effected without violence, or the suspension of the laws, or the closing of the courts.

The military power was nowhere placed above the civil authorities. None were seized and imprisoned at the mandate of arbitrary power: all divisions among the people disappeared, and the determination became unanimous that there should never again be any union with the northern States. Almost as one man, all who were able to bear arms rushed to the defence of an invaded country; and nowhere has it been found necessary to compel men to serve, or to enlist mercenaries by the offer of extraordinary bounties.

But in the northern States the Cherokee people saw with alarm a violated Constitution, all civil liberty put in peril, and all the rules of civilized warfare and the dictates of common humanity and decency unhesitatingly disregarded. In States which still adhered to the Union, a military despotism had displaced the civil power, and the laws became silent amid arms.

Free speech and almost free thought became a crime. The right to the writ of habeas corpus, guaranteed by the Constitution, disappeared at the nod of the Secretary of State or a general of the lowest grade. The mandate of the Chief Justice of the Supreme Court was set at naught by the military power, and this outrage on common right approved by a President sworn to support the Constitution. War on the largest scale was waged, and immense bodies of troops called into the field, in the absence of any law warranting it, under the pretence of suppressing unlawful combinations of men. The humanities of war which even barbarians respect were no longer thought worthy to be observed: foreign mercenaries and the scum of cities and the inmates of prisons were enlisted and organized into regiments and brigades, and sent into southern States to aid in subjugating a people struggling for freedom, to burn, to plunder, and to commit the basest of outrages on women.

While the heels of armed tyranny trod upon the necks of Maryland and Missouri, and men of the highest character and position were incarcerated, upon suspicion and without process of law, in jails, in forts, and in prison-ships, and even women were imprisoned by the arbitrary order of a President and cabinet ministers; while the press ceased to be free, the publication of newspapers was suspended, and their issues seized and destroyed; the officers and men taken prisoners in battle were allowed to remain in captivity by the refusal of their government to consent to an exchange of prisoners; as they had left their dead on more than one field of battle that had witnessed their defeat, to be buried, and their wounded to be cared for, by southern hands.

Whatever causes the Cherokee people may have had in the past to complain of some of the southern States, they cannot but feel that their interests and their destiny are inseparably connected with those of the south. The war now raging is a war of northern cupidity and fanaticism against the institution of African servitude, against the commercial freedom of the south, and against the political freedom of the States; and its objects are to annihilate the sovereignty of those States, and utterly change the nature of the general government.

The Cherokee people and their neighbors were warned before the war commenced that the first object of the party which now holds the powers of government of the United States would be to annul the institution of slavery in the whole Indian country, and make it what they term free territory, and after a time a free State. And they have been also warned, by the fate which has befallen those of their race in Kansas, Nebraska, and Oregon, that at no distant day they too would be compelled to surrender their country, at the demand of northern rapacity, and be content with an extinct nationality, and with reserves of limited extent for individuals, of which their people would soon be despoiled by speculators, if not plundered unscrupulously by the State.

Urged by these considerations, the Cherokees, long divided in opinion, became unanimous; and, like their brethren, the Creeks, Seminoles, Choctaws, and Chickasaws, determined by the undivided voice of a general convention of all the people, held at Tahlequah, on the 21st day of August in the present year, to make common cause with the south and share its fortunes.

In now carrying this resolution into effect, and consummating a treaty of alliance and friendship with the Confederate States of America, the Cherokee people declares that it has been faithful and loyal to its engagements with the United States, until, by placing its safety and even its national existence in imminent peril, those States have released them from those engagements. Menaced by a great danger, they exercise the inalienable right of self-defence, and declare themselves a free people, independent of the northern States of America, and at war with them by their own act. Obeying the dictates of prudence, and providing for the general safety and welfare, confident of the rectitude of their intentions, and true to the obligations of duty and honor, they accept the issue thus forced upon them, unite their fortunes now and forever with those of the Confederate States, and take up arms for the common cause; and with entire confidence in the justice of that cause and a firm reliance upon Divine Providence, will resolutely abide the consequences.

Tahlequah, C. N., October 28, 1861.

THOMAS PEGG,
President of National Committee.

JOSH. ROSS, *Clerk of National Committee.*

Concurred.   LACY MOUSE, *Speaker of Council.*

THOS. B. WOLF, *Clerk of Council.*

Approved.   JOHN ROSS.

No. 7.

John Ross's speech to Drew's regiment, December 19, 1862.

[The address of John Ross, principal chief of the Cherokee Nation, delivered at Fort Gibson, to John Drew's regiment of Cherokees, on the occasion of the defection of the regiment, on the eve of a battle

with Opoth-ye-hola, the leader of the non-conforming Creeks, 19th
December, 1862, written out the day following by myself, and believed to be exactly correct.—HERCULES MARTIN, *Interpreter.*]

FELLOW-CITIZENS, SOLDIERS AND FRIENDS: I appear before you this
evening for the purpose of making a few remarks, previous to intro-
ducing your friend, Colonel Cooper, the commander of the confederate
forces in the Indian country, who intends to address you.

A few nights ago I had occasion to address some of you on a very
strange and extraordinary occasion, and now that you are nearly all
present, I will necessarily have to repeat much that I then said. I
then told you of the difficulty caused in the nation by the disruption
of the United States, and the action taken by our neighboring States
and tribes in joining the southern confederacy, which had left us
alone, and of other matters of equal interest, that made it necessary
for us to call a convention of the Cherokee people.

This convention was held and numerously attended by the people,
so that the acts of the convention were really the acts of the whole
people. At that convention it was agreed on that all the distinctions
of color should cease amongst the Cherokees forever, and that the
half-blood Cherokee should have equal rights and privileges with the
full-blood Cherokee, and the full-blood have the same rights and
privileges as their white-skinned brethren, and that the whole were
to be a united people. It was also agreed on, that, for the interests
of the nation, our relations with the United States should cease, or
be changed, for the reasons I have stated, and a treaty be made with
the south. For this purpose I was then authorized to enter into
negotiations with the commissioner of the southern confederacy,
with the view of making such a treaty. At the same time and for
this purpose there were men, in whom we had unbounded confidence,
selected to negotiate and enter into a treaty with the south.

Immediately after the convention I despatched a messenger to the
distinguished commissioner for the Confederate States, who was then
in the neighborhood of Fort * * *, and informed him of our readiness
to enter into a treaty. In the mean time, although there was no treaty
made, it was deemed expedient to raise a Cherokee regiment for our
own preservation, and for the purpose of repelling invasion and guard-
ing our own border, and in any emergency of this kind to act in con-
cert with the troops of the southern confederacy.

This regiment was accordingly raised and organized at this place.
On the arrival of the commissioner at this place, the regiment welcomed him, and formed his escort to his headquarters at Park Hill,
where the treaty was made. The treaty was made to the entire satisfaction of all who were concerned in it. It is the very best treaty
we have ever made in many particulars, as it secures to us advantages we have long sought, and gives us the rights of freemen to dis-
pose of our lands as we please. On the very day the treaty was
signed it was submitted to the national council, then in session, and
was then read and deliberated on, article by article, and unanimously
adopted and confirmed by both houses, and it thus became a law.
By negotiating this alliance with the Confederate States, we are

under obligations to aid the south against all its enemies, so that the enemies of the south are our enemies. * * * * *

Under these circumstances, the commissioner deemed it expedient to accept of this regiment into the service at once. This was only delayed by the absence of the officer who was authorized to muster them into the service, the late Colonel McIntosh, C. S. A., he having gone to duty under General McCulloch; but on learning this, Colonel Cooper sent another officer, who mustered them into the service, where the regiment has been since then, until the recent very strange, unaccountable blunder and confusion, when it acted as it did, when it was brought against Opoth-ye-hola's people a few days ago, which conduct has been examined into to-day and settled so advantageously by Colonel Cooper, the commander of the forces on this frontier, feeling assured that it was evidently caused by a misconception of matters as they really exist, or a mistake and misunderstanding of what Opoth-le-hola really is. When we concluded to enter into (a treaty) negotiations with the Confederate States, by request of the commissioner, I sent a messenger to the Osages and Senecas, requesting them to meet the commissioner at Park Hill, and they very promptly responded. I also despatched a messenger to Opoth-le-hola for the same purpose, and advised him to submit to the treaty made with the Creeks, and to be advised by Colonel Cooper, who was his friend, and had used his utmost exertions to bring about peaceful relations with the parties in the Creek Nation. Opoth-le-hola replied that he was at peace with the south, with Colonel Cooper, and the Cherokees, and desired to remain so. He was willing also to submit to all proper treaties, but that a party in his own nation was against him and his people, who would not allow him to be at peace.

On this I used every possible means to settle the disputes between the parties and bring about a peace, and hoped to succeed. The very last messenger Opoth-le-hola sent to me, one of his chiefs, * * * asked for my advice and intervention. I then sent a letter by the same messenger to Colonel Cooper, expressive of my views, and sent back word to Opoth-ye-hola to come alone into the Cherokee country, where he would be protected, and to disperse his people and send them to their homes, and by no means to fight. But, instead of doing this, he comes into the Cherokee country with a large armed force, and wantonly destroys the stock and other property of our citizens: by this means, without cause, invading our soil, and proving our enemy. He, by his subtlety, seeks to inveigle the Cherokees into his quarrel, as he still tells them he was their friend, but proving by his duplicity that he is not, as shown by his acts, for, while pretending peace, he was preparing for war, and has been deceiving us all the time, and no doubt has his agents amongst you, deluding you into the belief that it was only a party feud, and that he was oppressed, while he was acting for the north all the time. The very last messenger sent to him by Colonel Drew was at his own request, yet with the full authority of Colonel Cooper, and Colonel D. N. McIntosh was charged with offers of peace, and this was from the

3

leader of the very party he complained of, yet the messenger was intercepted and prevented from seeing Opoth-le-hola by some of his chiefs or officers who were already stripped and painted for war.

It was this state of things that produced the strange blunder of this occasion and caused the separation of the regiment. Our treaty with the south is a good one, and, as I said, is the best we have ever made, securing many advantages we did not before possess; it is therefore our duty and interest to respect it, and we must, as the interest of our common country demands it. According to the stipulations of the treaty we must fight the enemies of our allies, whenever the south requires it, as they are our enemies as well as the enemies of the south; and I feel sure that no such occurrence as the one we deplore would have taken place if all things were understood as I have endeavored to explain them. Indeed, the true meaning of our treaty is, that we must know no line in the presence of our invader, be he who he may. We must not let the invader carry the war into our land, but meet him before he reaches our lines and repel him. If, unfortunately, the invader should cross our lines, we must expel him by force, with the aid of our allies, and pursue him into his own country, as this is the intent of our treaty. For, although we were more specially to be the guards of our own border, and are not required to go a long distance from our homes to fight the battles of the south, yet we are not restricted to a line when there is an enemy in view, but must repel him, pursue and destroy him. I hope you now understand it, and that everything will now go on well, as it should. I have no more to say, and will now introduce Colonel Cooper, the commander of the confederate forces in the Indian country.

The Cherokees gave their customary token of approval, when they were addressed by Colonel Cooper to the same effect as J. Ross. They were then addressed in the Cherokee language by Major T. Pegg, at some length, but this was not interpreted. Many of the regiment left for their homes that night, not approving of the treaty and its requirements.

The foregoing is almost verbatim, and contains at least the substance of all the chief said.

W. L. G. MILLER.

No. 8.

John Ross to General Albert Pike, January 1, 1862.

PARK HILL, CHEROKEE NATION, *January 1, 1862.*

SIR: Thinking that you may have arrived at Fort Gibson by this time, I beg leave to inform you that your communication, with the amendments to the Cherokee treaty, has been received. The national council has been convened for Monday next, in extra session, for the purpose of taking into consideration those amendments. If conve-

nient to visit us on that occasion, it will afford me great pleasure
to welcome you as a guest at my house.

I have the honor to be, very respectfully and truly, your obedient
servant,

JOHN ROSS,
Principal Chief Cherokee Nation.

Brigadier General A. PIKE, *C. S. A.*

Original on file in this office.

D. N. COOLEY.
Commissioner Indian Affairs.

No. 9.

John Ross to General Pike, February 25, 1862.

EXECUTIVE DEPARTMENT,
Park Hill, February 25, 1862.

SIR : I have deemed it my duty to address you on the present occasion. You have doubtless ere this received my communication, enclosing the action of the national council with regard to the final ratification of our treaty. Colonel Drew's regiment promptly took up the line of march, on the receipt of your order from Fort Smith, towards Fayetteville. I accompanied the troops some twelve miles east of this, and I am happy to assure you in the most confident manner that in my opinion this regiment will not fail to do their whole duty, whenever the conflict with the common enemy shall take place. There are so many conflicting reports as to your whereabouts, and consequently much interest is felt by the people to know where the headquarters of your military operations will be established during the present emergencies. I had intended going up to see the troops of our regiment; also to visit the headquarters of the army at Cane Hill, in view of affording every aid in any manner within the reach of my power to repel the enemy. But I am sorry to say I have been dissuaded from going at present, in consequence of some unwarrantable conduct on the part of many base, reckless and unprincipled persons belonging to Watie's regiment, who are under no subordination or restraint of their leaders, in domineering over and trampling upon the rights of peaceable and unoffending citizens. I have at all times in the most unequivocal manner assured the people that you will not only promptly discountenance, but will take steps to put a stop to such proceedings, for the protection of their persons and property, and to redress their wrongs. This is not the time for crimination and recrimination ; at a proper time I have certain specific complaints to report for your investigation. Pardon me for again reiterating, that the mass of the people are all right in sentiment for the support of the treaty of alliance with the Confederate States.   I shall be happy to hear from you.

I have the honor to be your obedient servant,

JOHN ROSS,
Principal Chief Cherokee Nation.

Brigadier General A. PIKE,
    Commanding Indian Department.

Original on file in this office.

D. N. COOLEY,
Commissioner Indian Affairs.

No. 10.

John Ross to General Pike, March 22, 1862.

EXECUTIVE DEPARTMENT,
Park Hill, C. N., March 22, 1862.

SIR: I respectfully beg leave to invite your attention to the exposed condition of the northern and almost entire eastern border of the Cherokee Nation. Since the battles of the 7th and 8th instant in Benton county, Ark., there is no force to withstand the invasion of the federal army if it should meet their policy to move either in force or by detached parties into the Cherokee country. This state of affairs naturally begets apprehension and anxiety in the minds of the people, and which, fanned by false reports that are in constant circulation, may degenerate into a panic. The funds of the nation and all its public records are wholly unprotected and at the mercy not only of federal reconnoitring parties, but of even a few lawless individuals, if they should combine under such favorable circumstances for plunder and mischief. My object in addressing you this note is, therefore, in a most respectful manner to request that Colonel Drew's regiment, or a portion of it, be stationed in this immediate vicinity to afford whatever protection may be in their power to the public property of the nation, and to be used as scouts for the benefit of the army and the citizens of the nation in keeping up reliable information as to the movement of the United States forces. I have no reliable information of the proximity of any federal troops, although reports are circulating to that effect. I have just returned from Tahlequah, and could not learn certainly that any have been at Cincinnati on the line. Rev. Young Ewing, who came down last evening from the vicinity of Evansville, where he had been for a day or two, heard that the federal army was about the battle-ground and its vicinity, and that Missourians in larger or smaller numbers were coming down the line road to join General Price's army. Should any information be received by me before to-morrow morning entitled to credit, I will forward it by officers of the regiment, who will be proceeding to Webber's Falls in the morning.

I have the honor to be, sir, very respectfully, your obedient servant,

JOHN ROSS,
Principal Chief Cherokee Nation.

Brigadier General A. PIKE,
Commanding Indian Department.

Original on file in this office.

D. N. COOLEY.
Commissioner Indian Affairs.

No. 11.

John Ross to , *March* 21, 1862.

EXECUTIVE DEPARTMENT,
Park Hill, C. N., March 21, 1862.

SIR: I am in receipt of your favor of the 23d inst. I have no doubt that forage can be procured for Colonel Drew's men in this vicinity by hauling it in from the farms of the surrounding districts. The subject of a delegate in congress shall be attended to so soon as arrangements can be made for holding an election. I am happy to learn that Colonel Drew has been authorized to furlough a portion of the men in his regiment to raise corn. I shall endeavor to be correctly informed of the movement of the enemy, and to advise you of the same, and I shall be gratified to receive any important information that you may have to communicate at all times.

I am, very respectfully and truly, yours, &c.,
JOHN ROSS,
Principal Chief Cherokee Nation.

Original on file in this office.

D. N. C., *Commissioner of Indian Affairs.*

No. 12.

John Ross to General Pike, April 10, 1862.

EXECUTIVE DEPARTMENT,
Park Hill, C. N., April 10, 1862.

SIR: I beg leave to thank you for your kind response to my letter of the 22d ultimo, and your order stationing Colonel Drew's regiment in this vicinity. Though much reduced by furloughs, in number, it will be useful for the particular purposes for which it was ordered here. The unprotected condition of the country, however, is a source of general anxiety among the people, who feel that they are liable to be overrun at any time by small parties from the United States army, which remains in the vicinity of the late battle-ground. This is more particularly the case since the removal of the confederate forces under your command, and those under Major General Price. Without distrusting the wisdom that has prompted these movements, or the manifestation of any desire on my part to inquire into their policy, it will be, nevertheless, a source of satisfaction to be able to assure the people of the country that protection will not be withheld from them, and that they will not be left to their own feeble defence. Your response is respectfully requested.

I have the honor to be, sir, with high regard, your obedient servant.

JOHN ROSS,
Principal Chief Cherokee Nation.

Brig. Gen. A. PIKE.
        Com'y Department Indian Territory,
        Headquarters Choctaw Nation.

Original on file in this office.
D. N. C., Commissioner of Indian Affairs.

No. 13.

Letter of T. J. Mackey, June 4, 1866.

WASHINGTON, D. C., June 4, 1866.

SIR: In compliance with your request, I have the honor to submit the following statement in regard to the alliance between the Cherokee Nation and the late Confederate States.

In May of 1861 the Cherokee Nation issued a declaration of neutrality in view of the war then begun between the United States and the Confederate States. That declaration was concurred in by the confederate authorities, and it was respected by General McCulloch, who commanded an army of about eight thousand (8,000) confederates on the eastern border of the Cherokee country. This neutrality was maintained until the battle of Wilson's Creek, in which the forces of the United States were defeated, on the 9th day of August, 1861. Soon after that battle John Ross, the principal chief of the Cherokees, announced to General Pike, the commissioner empowered by the Confederate States to treat with the several Indian nations, that the Cherokees were ready to renounce their neutrality and enter into an alliance, offensive and defensive, with the Confederate States. A treaty was effected on this basis. The Confederate States bound themselves to pay the sum of two hundred and fifty thousand dollars ($250,000) to the Cherokees on the ratification of the treaty; to continue the annuities that they had formerly received from the United States, and to indemnify them for all losses that might accrue to them in consequence of their abrogating their treaties with the United States. The Cherokees, through their chief John Ross, bound themselves to furnish all their able-bodied men to the Confederate States for service against the United States; and it was stipulated that the

Cherokee forces should not be required to march out of their own territory without their special consent. Pursuant to that treaty a force of Cherokees was organized under the direction of John Ross. A portion of this force, consisting of Cherokees of the old Ross or Pin party, was in the battle of Pea Ridge or Elkhorn, where they killed and scalped the wounded of the federal army. This fact was made the subject of a correspondence between Major General Curtis, of the United States army and General Pike. That battle was fought in March, 1862.

In July of 1862 Colonel Weir, of the United States army, commanding a force on the northern border of the Cherokee country, sent a communication to Ross, proposing that the Cherokees should annul their treaty with the Confederate States and form an alliance with the United States; and Colonel Weir invited his attention to the fact that the confederate authorities had violated their treaty with the Cherokees by withdrawing all their forces from the Cherokee country. He offered John Ross, and such chiefs as he might designate, a safe-conduct through his lines to Washington and return. This proposition was declined peremptorily by Ross, who declared that the Cherokees disdained an alliance with a people who had authorized and practiced the most monstrous barbarities in violation of the laws of war; that the Cherokees were bound to the Confederate States by the faith of treaties and by a community of sentiment and interest; that they were born upon the soil of the south, and would stand or fall with the States of the south. This reply, with an explanatory letter, was sent to General Pike by Ross, in charge of Ross's son. I was chief engineer of the Indian department at the time, and read them. General Pike was then encamped at Fort McCulloch, in the Chickasaw Nation.

About three months after Ross penned this reply to Colonel Weir he went over to the United States, with a little over a half of the Cherokees, embracing the greater portion of the full-bloods.

I am, sir, very respectfully, your obedient servant,

T. J. MACKEY.

Hon. D. N. Cooley,
Commissioner Indian Affairs, Washington, D. C.

A.

Message of the principal chief of the Cherokee Nation to the national committee and council in national council convened.

FRIENDS AND FELLOW-CITIZENS: Since the last meeting of the national council, events have occurred that will occupy a prominent place in the history of the world. The United States have been dissolved, and two governments now exist. Twelve of the States composing the late Union have erected themselves into a government under the style of the Confederate States of America, and, as you know, are now engaged in a war for their independence. The con-

test thus far has been attended with success, almost uninterrupted, on
their side, and marked by brilliant victories. Of its final result there
seems to be no ground for a reasonable doubt. The unanimity and
devotion of the people of the Confederate States must sooner or later
secure their success over all opposition, and result in the establish-
ment of their independence and a recognition of it by the other
nations of the earth. At the beginning of the conflict, I felt that the
interests of the Cherokee people would be best maintained by remaining quiet and not involving themselves in it prematurely. Our
relations had long existed with the United States government, and
bound us to observe amity and peace alike with all the States. Neutrality was proper and wise so long as there remained a reasonable
probability that the difficulty between the two sections of the Union
would be settled, as a different course would have placed all our
rights in jeopardy and might have led to the sacrifice of the people.
But when there was no longer any reason to believe that the Union
of the States would be continued, there was no cause to hesitate as to
the course the Cherokee Nation should pursue. Our geographical
position and domestic institutions allied us to the south, while the
developments daily made in our vicinity as to the purposes of the war
waged against the Confederate States clearly pointed out the path of interest. These considerations produced a unanimity of sentiment among
the people as to the policy to be adopted by the Cherokee Nation,
which was clearly expressed in their general meeting held at Tahlequah on the 21st day of August last. A copy of the proceedings of
that meeting is submitted for your information. In accordance with
the declarations embodied in the resolutions then adopted, the executive council deemed it proper to exercise the authority conferred
upon them by the people there assembled. Messengers were despatched to General Albert Pike, the distinguished Indian commissioner
of the Confederate States, who, having negotiated treaties with the
neighboring Indian nations, was then establishing relations between
his government and the Comanches and other Indians in the southwest, who bore a copy of the proceedings of the meeting referred to,
and a letter from the executive authorities, proposing on behalf of
the nation to enter into a treaty of alliance, defensive and offensive,
with the Confederate States. In the exercise of the same general
authority, and to be ready, as far as practicable, to meet any emergency that might spring up on our northern border, it was thought proper to raise a regiment of mounted men, and tender its service to General McCulloch. The people responded with alacrity to the call, and
it is believed the regiment will be found as efficient as any other like
number of men. It is now in the service of the Confederate States,
for the purpose of aiding in defending their homes and the common
rights of the Indian nations about us. This regiment is composed of
ten full companies, with two reserve companies, and, in addition to
the force previously authorized to be raised to operate outside of the
nation by General McCulloch, will show that the Cherokee people are
ready to do all in their power in defence of the confederate cause,
which has now become their own.

And it is to be hoped that our people will spare no means to sustain them, but contribute liberally to supply any want of comfortable clothing for the approaching season. In years long since past, our ancestors met undaunted those who would invade their mountain homes beyond the Mississippi; let not their descendants of the present day be found unworthy of them, or unable to stand by the chivalrous men of the south by whose side they may be called to fight in self-defence. The Cherokee people do not desire to be involved in war, but self-preservation fully justifies them in the course they have adopted, and they will be recreant to themselves if they should not sustain it to the utmost of their humble abilities.

A treaty with the Confederate States has been entered into and is now submitted for your ratification. In view of the circumstances by which we are surrounded, and the provisions of the treaty, it will be found to be the most important ever negotiated on behalf of the Cherokee Nation, and will mark a new era in its history. Without attempting a recapitulation of all its provisions, some of its distinguishing features may be briefly enumerated. The relations of the Cherokee Nation are changed from the United to the Confederate States, with guarantees of protection, and a recognition in future negotiations only of its constitutional authorities. The metes and boundaries as defined by patent from the United States are continued, and a guaranty given for the neutral land, or a fair consideration in case it should be lost by war or negotiation, and an advance thereon to pay the national debt, and to meet other contingencies. The payment of all our annuities and the security of our investments are provided for. The jurisdiction of the Cherokee courts over all members of the nation, whether by birth, marriage, or adoption, is recognized.

Our title to our lands is placed beyond dispute. Our relations with the Confederate States is that of a ward; theirs to us that of a protectorate with powers restricted. The district court, with a limited civil and criminal jurisdiction, is admitted into the country instead of being located in Van Buren, as was the United States court. This is, perhaps, one of the most important provisions of the treaty, and secures to our own citizens the great constitutional right of trial by a jury of their vicinage, and releases them from the petty abuses and vexations of the old system before a foreign jury and in a foreign country. It gives us a delegate in Congress on the same footing with delegates from the Territories, by which our interests can be represented—a right which has long been withheld from the nation, and which has imposed upon it a large expense and great injustice. It also contains reasonable stipulation in regard to the appointment and powers of the agent, and in regard to licensed traders. The Cherokee Nation may be called upon to furnish troops for the defence of the Indian country, but is never to be taxed for the support of any war in which the States may be engaged.

The Cherokee people stand upon new ground. Let us hope that the clouds which overspread the land will be dispersed, and that we shall prosper as we have never before done. New avenues to usefulness and distinction will be opened to the ingenuous youth of the country. Our rights of self-government will be more fully recognized, and our citizens be no longer dragged off upon flimsy pretexts to be imprisoned and tried before distant tribunals. No just cause exists for domestic difficulties. Let them be buried with the past, and only mutual friendship and harmony be cherished.

Our relations with the neighboring tribes are of the most friendly character. Let us see that the white path which leads from our country to theirs be obstructed by no act of ours, and that it be open to all those with whom we may be brought into intercourse.

Amid the excitement of the times, it is to be hoped that the interests of education will not be allowed to suffer, and that no interruption be brought into the usual operations of the government. Let all its officers continue to discharge their appropriate duties. As the services of some of your members may be required elsewhere, and all unnecessary expense should be avoided, I respectfully recommend that the business of the session be promptly discharged.

JNO. ROSS.

EXECUTIVE DEPARTMENT, *Tahlequah. C. N.. Oct.* 9, 1861.

B.

Statement of the commissioner to the northern Cherokees as to what points the government would insist upon.

1st. A provision that the Cherokees (northern) have a country north of the Arkansas, and in the eastern part of the "Cherokee country," east of the Grand river, below Ross's ford, and so far west above that line, extending to the north line of the Indian country, as is equal to 320 acres for each Cherokee man, woman, and child, and 80 acres for each person of color, formerly a slave to any Cherokee, who may remain in said country.

2d. Such Cherokees as may, on account of former feuds and such difficulties as now exist in the nation, and who now live in the Canadian district, or west of Grand river, and east of 95° 30′ west longitude, and such as may go into that district within one year to reside, shall each have for his and their use 160 acres of land for each Cherokee, and 80 acres for each freedman, formerly slave of such Cherokee. They shall have their pro rata share of the school funds, equal rights in the benefits of academies and seminaries, and   dollars out of the avails of the sale of territory to the United States, and their equitable proportion of the funds of the nation: and while they remain in such separate territory, the Cherokee national authorities shall have no jurisdiction over them; but so far as their dealings with the United States are concerned, they shall be considered part of the Cherokee Nation; and in case the two portions of the Cherokees shall hereafter so determine, they shall be reunited.

3d. A census of the Cherokees in the nation. and of those outside in the districts above named, shall be taken within a year, under direction of the agent.

4th. The improvements of those in the districts above named, belonging to such Cherokees as may within one year desire to return to the Cherokee country east of the Grand river and north of the Arkansas, shall be paid for by those who remove into the first-named districts.

5th. The laws of the Cherokees providing for confiscation of property to be void, and their improvements to be restored to such as decide to return to their homes.

6th. A general amnesty for all offences growing out of the late rebellion.

7th. The United States to purchase the neutral lands at a fair price.

8th. Texas and North Carolina Cherokees to have the same rights as other Cherokees, if they remove and live with them upon their reservations.

9th. Consent to be given to a territorial government on the principle of Senate bill 459. 38th Congress.

10th. The freedmen to be dealt with as liberally as in the case of Choctaws and Chickasaws.

11th. Right of way to be given for railroads in either direction.

12th. Sale to the United States of lands lying west of 95° 30′ west longitude.

C.

Conference between Hon. D. N. Cooley, Commissioner of Indian Affairs, and northern Cherokees, May 5, 1866, (Mr. Ewing, attorney for northern Cherokees ; Mr. Voorhees, attorney for southern Cherokees.)

Mr. COOLEY. We do not want the land you offer, unless you give us some east of 97° with it.

Mr. EWING. That subject was so thoroughly discussed at our last meeting that it is unnecessary to spend time on it now.

Captain BANGS. Our intentions have been understood.

Mr. COOLEY. Then I understand you will not go east of 97 . Have you any further propositions to make in relation to southern Cherokees? Have you thought about settling another district?

(The delegation here submitted a letter purporting to show that most of the southern refugees had returned to their homes.)

Mr. VOORHEES. Read it. (It was read.) Suppose the delegation could be convinced that there are not 200 back in the country, what would they do?

Mr. EWING, (waiving the question.) We want to make a treaty now, or go home. We have been here a long time without accomplishing the object for which we came.

Mr. COOLEY. I have no idea that so many have returned.

Mr. VOORHEES. They went to the Canadian district, a great many of them. to raise a crop for this year.

Mr. COOLEY. The only object of the department is to make them self-sustaining and peaceable. That many have taken the oath and gone to their old homes we have no positive evidence.

Mr. D. H. Ross reads letter from H. D. Rees, which says the refugees are going to the Canadian district.

Mr. Cooley. I believe that. The military were ordered to protect them there.

Mr. Voorhees. If these men were going home to live we would not spend our time here trying to get a separation.

Mr. Ewing (reads, interrupting.) "General Watie wants to break up the Cherokee Nation."

Mr. Voorhees. We could bring bushels of letters, but we do not want to make personal attacks.

Mr. Cooley. I am for business.

Mr. Ewing. We expected a proposition from you.

Mr. Cooley. What of a proposition to settle them between Verdigris and Arkansas, or Little Verdigris and Arkansas, west of 95½°?

Mr. Ewing. I think they will agree to settle them west of the Little Verdigris.

Mr. Cooley. That takes the river and timber off.

Mr. Ewing. No, not altogether.

Mr. Cooley. There is land enough east of Grand river for Cherokees. We are making a treaty with Delawares and other Kansas Indians, and they want to get together. I do not think your proposition opens up any inducements to Kansas Indians.

Mr. Ewing. These men, after several months of deliberation, have decided to cede no lands east of 97°, nor to allow any other tribes with them unless they consent to live under their laws.

Captain Benge. We don't want two governments for a small tribe of Indians. I think they ought to yield some.

Mr. Cooley. They come here merely asking for what they want. They make no demands. If you cannot agree, we must put a government there. I am in favor of your project in regard to the Kansas Indians, but none of these bands appear willing to assent.

Mr. Voorhees. The point upon which we are most solicitous is this one of jurisdiction. If they are to hold the sway and domineering power over us, we have no guarantee the bygone scenes of bloodshed will not be re-enacted.

Mr. Ewing. If these people are settled fifty or sixty miles away it will stop that.

Mr. Voorhees. Will you let us make our own laws?

Mr. Ewing. No.

Col. Phillips. Colonel Adair said yesterday "they were not whipped;" and I believe the spirit of disloyalty lingers in them yet as bad as ever.

(After a debate on that remark, amounting to nothing)—

Mr. Voorhees. We don't want to destroy the unity of the nation. Give us our council, courts, laws, local judges, &c., and let the government deal with us as one people, in proportion to numbers, and if after a time our people are willing to coalesce, we will be glad of it.

Mr. Cooley. Is there any probability of this delegation adopting such a plan?

Mr. EWING. No, not a bit.

Mr. VOORHEES. What, except the mere love of power, could induce you to want to exercise such jurisdiction over us as that?

Mr. COOLEY. The Choctaws and Chickasaws are living peacefully under their treaty.

Mr. EWING. They are of different blood.

Mr. VOORHEES. I have talked with many prominent men, who know the state of affairs in that country, and not one of them believes the southern Cherokees will go back to their old homes and live. I say with the utmost sincerity there is not one but would be perfectly satisfied to go to their homes if they believed they would be fairly dealt with.

Col. PHILLIPS. They were one nation before.

Mr. COOLEY. The proposition to protect these men in their rights is proper. They are willing to yield some of their rights. They make no demands. If there is the danger the other delegates say, that they will do some night as their fathers did, I should be very sorry.

Mr. VOORHEES. The government cannot extend protection where there is a disposition among Indians to injure.

Mr. EWING. That gives the Cherokees a character I do not think they deserve. They lived in absolute peace from 1846 to 1861.

Mr. VOORHEES. I don't want to harrow up these things, except to show that they really did happen. Judge Tibbetts said murders were common.

Mr. JONES then related the list of murders in detail, and the causes, from 1846 to 1861, as near as the delegation could remember.

Mr. VOORHEES. Did not a feud break up the schools and churches before the war?

Mr. EWING. Yes.

Mr. VOORHEES. Disloyalty is a misnomer. We present a plan, by which there can be no possibility of a renewal of troubles. Let us have a place apart, live separate, and be governed separately, but come here and treat together as the Cherokee Nation.

Mr. EWING. White rebels would like such a plan.

Mr. VOORHEES. These people are not, like the people of the south, getting their homes back and being protected in them. They would be glad to get such treatment.

Mr. EWING. You ask a separation on account of your disloyalty.

Mr. VOORHEES. That is a misfortune, and not a merit. Why do you still persist in wanting to dictate our laws to us when you will live far away from us, and will not know what laws are peculiarly adapted to us?

Mr. JONES. The reason why we hold that point so tenaciously is because we feel we have a responsibility there. We have this interest at heart.

Mr. COOLEY. What about the money provision in article 7?

Mr. EWING. The Secretary suggested about $100. He don't want much inducement offered.

Mr. COOLEY. I should not much like such a plan. I did not know that was the Secretary's feeling in the matter.

Mr. Jones. I think only a few will go west. The rest will settle at their old homes.

Mr. Cooley. I don't think any Cherokee should be driven west of 98°.

Captain Benge. We won't divide.

Mr. Cooley. Unless you make a more liberal proposition I will recommend another.

Captain Benge. We will not do it; we cannot; we will not make any further concessions.

Mr. Cooley. Do you wish those words recorded?

Mr. Ewing. No; don't put them down.

Mr. Cooley. In regard to the cession of land, if you will not cede any east of the Arkansas it is useless to argue the point further.

Mr. Ewing. I don't think the delegation could be got to cede any land east of the Arkansas; but if we can get these Kansas Indians to move down there under such an arrangement as we have named, it would suit all.

Mr. Cooley. The next meeting I will have a proposition as a *sine qua non*. I have none now. (Reads letter from General Blunt in relation to Cherokees.) General Blunt says it is impracticable, on account of a bitter feud, to have them live together under the same jurisdiction. Thinks they will not live together.

Mr. Cooley. It seems to be the desire to put railroads in that country. All other treaties provide certain interest in the lands to the railroad companies, and I think it would be better for the Cherokees.

Mr. Ewing. They don't want to do it. They are afraid the railroad companies will sell the land to white men.

Mr. Cooley. All other treaties have provision in them that none but Indians shall be allowed to purchase the land.

Mr. Jones. The Secretary said in regard to the railroad question: "You might do it, but I don't advise you to give them any land."

Mr. Cooley. Do you think your people would give the southern Cherokees a separate district and allow them local jurisdiction?

Mr. Ewing. The law allows them a district judge; that is all we will guarantee. As an evidence of the death of feuds prior to the war, Mr. Standwatie was president of council, Colonel Adair was a member of the upper house, and other prominent men in them were in various positions of honor under the Cherokee government.

Mr. Cooley. We do not recognize Standwatie as chief of the Cherokees; we recognize him as chief of a council. These southern Cherokees say they are afraid to go back. Their demands are not unreasonable, except as to breaking up the government. Why not give them a district to suit them, and let them have their own local magistrates?

Colonel Phillips. It is not so much separating the country as separating the government.

Mr. Jones. We would much rather take in Indians and not sell land.

Mr. Cooley. I shall probably be able on Tuesday to say what the government will ask.

Adjourned until Tuesday, May 8.

I.

Letter from Judge Harlan, Cherokee agent, to Commissioner of Indian Affairs.

WASHINGTON, D. C., *March* 28. 1866.

SIR: Yours of this date received. I have the honor to answer:

The number of the Cherokee people, according to the most reliable data within my reach, is about 17,000.

This is, however, but an estimate, never having been able to obtain a census of even that part of the nation which remained in the nation after the rebellion. In the issue of provisions and clothing to that portion which remained, I kept a register of those receiving aid. I issued food and clothing only to old men, women and children. These amounted to about 9,000. When the army was disbanded nearly 1,500, soldiers were mustered out of the service, which, together with the women, children, and old men. make 10,500. Of the Watie party which went south, I have still less upon which to form an opinion. That party had left the nation before I got there. But from what I learn from many sources—and I have made much inquiry—I suppose the Watie party to number about 6,500.

This party, at present, is scattered over a large tract of country between Red river and the Arkansas.

That part of the Cherokee country lying southwest of the Arkansas river, and between Forts Smith and Gibson, at the breaking out of the rebellion, was partially settled. Exposed sometimes to one side and then to the other, neither party could occupy it. Both abandoned it. Some went south, and the balance crossed the Arkansas river to the northeast. Into that part thus abandoned I am told the Watie party are now returning. in what numbers I cannot certainly say ; from what I learn. I judge not in very great numbers—to the first day of January last under one hundred. I suppose there are more now. The number returned to the northeast side of the Arkansas to the same date was about one hundred. That number has been increased since. but the extent I have no reliable information—I think not very largely.

You ask me my opinion of the probability of the Waity and Ross party being reconciled and living together in peace.

At Fort Smith, last fall, I conversed freely with both parties. From the spirit manifested by both. I did not then think they could : I still remain of the same opinion. Their feud dates back forty years, it grew more fierce at the treaty in 1835: still more fierce in 1839, when so many were assassinated of the Ridge party. This great slaughter weakened the Ridge party, but it did not make the friends of those slaughtered love the slayers. They do not now, and never will. A slight cause, real or imaginary, and the fires of the ancient feud will blaze forth as fiercely as it ever did. An attempt is now being made to show that the feud is forgotten or forgiven. I hope it is so, but in the three years I have lived in the nation I have received no evidence which has led me to hope that if they reunite the bloody scenes of 1839 will not be re-enacted. They had not made friends to the outbreak of the rebellion. Nothing has, of course, transpired since to mollify the hate that so long existed. Those who know the Indian character best are the most confident that peace between the parties is impossible. I may be wrong, but that is my opinion. This was the opinion of both parties last fall at Fort Smith. The Watie party then thought they would not be secure if they returned. At that time, and to this time, as far as I know, the Ross party were determined that a considerable portion of the Watie party should not be secure if they did return; and so far as I know, the determination still exists. The Ross party now say they can live in peace—I hope they can; it is only my hope, not my belief. If the Cherokees agree to do so, I see no reason why the United States government should object. The Indians are the only parties particularly interested.

I will make one further observation: both parties of the Cherokee Nation are now here represented. I see nothing in their conduct here towards each other tending to convince me that the old feud is not just as fresh and violent as it ever has been, or ever can be.

With great respect, your obedient servant,

J. HARLAN, *U. S. Indian Agent.*

ELIJAH SELLS,
Sup't of Indian Affairs, Southern Superintendency.

J.

Letter from Hon. J. M. Tebbetts to Commissioner of Indian Affairs.

WASHINGTON, D. C., *March* 30, 1866.

SIR: I am in receipt of your communication of this date, in which you request me to furnish your office with any information I may possess in relation to the condition of the Cherokees, both northern and southern, especially as regards the probability of their reuniting, and living together as one people, together with any views and suggestions which may be of service to the government in arranging the difficulties between them.

I have no means at the present time of estimating the number of northern and southern Cherokees; but I am of opinion that the estimate of Superindendent Sells will be found to approximate the true number. The great body of the southern Cherokees are now home-less on Red river; some, pressed by hunger, are hanging on the borders of the Cherokee territory, to receive the rations distributed by government at Fort Gibson, and awaiting the action of the government here; others, very few in number, have returned to their old homes.

I have been residing since 1839 in Arkansas, immediately on the frontier. My opportunity for learning their condition and party relations has been good. I have long been impressed with the idea that the policy of the government towards this people, in one respect especially, has been a most signal failure—a policy, however well intended, which has wholly failed to secure to them the most important guarantees of the treaty of 1835; a policy which has resulted in feuds and broils, rapine and murder, and, if continued, will result in the extermination of one or the other of the hostile factions.

It is a great mistake to suppose that these dissentions are of a recent date; they go back to the treaty of 1835, and are as irradicable as the traditions of that haughty race. By the treaty 1817 a portion of this great tribe emigrated west of the Mississippi, and settled on territory now embraced within the limits of the State of Arkansas. By the treaty of 1828 those remaining behind, in the State of Georgia, were guaranteed the quiet and undisturbed possession of that country forever. But the restless and aggressive white man pressed upon them, and the State of Georgia, insisting on the boundaries embraced in the royal charter, extended her laws and jurisdiction over this people. Then arose the memorable conflict between the State of Georgia and the Cherokee Nation, involving the general government in complications from which it sought to extricate itself by the treaty of 1835. An earnest appeal was made to the eastern Cherokees to cede all their lands and remove west of the Mississippi. They hesitated long. Here were the graves of their sires; here were their homes and their hunting-grounds. Every hill and valley, rivulet, and glen, had its tradition, and told of deeds of daring and renown. Here were their affections; this was their home. But the white man still pressed, and the demands of the government were urgent; arguments and considerations were used which only the rich and powerful can use, and terms were accepted which only the weak and defenceless can accept. A majority of the eastern Cherokees refused to treat; a minority, however, seeing their hapless condition east of the Mississippi—State law and State jurisdiction invading their territory at every point, and strongly urged by the general government, accompanied with most sacred pledges of protection, entered into the treaty of New Echota, 1835, and, ceding their lands east, removed west of the Mississippi. These confiding men who made this treaty, and their adherents, are the same men who, with their wives and children, shivering in the cold, are now hovering on the borders of the Cherokee Nation, without shelter and without a home. Among the signers of this treaty will be found the names of Elias Boudinot, George W. Adair, and Stand Watie. These men, after the lapse of thirty years, are here again before the government, insisting upon the observance of that faith and the assurance of that protection so solemnly guaranteed in the treaty. The last is here in person; the former two are represented here by their sons, Elias C. Boudinot and William Penn Adair. They made this treaty in pursuance of the urgent wishes of the government. The non-treaty-making party were the most numerous. Here is the initial point of the deadly feuds and hatred between the treaty and the non-treaty parties, which have continued from 1835 down to the present time without surcease or intermission, resulting in rapine, murder, and assassination, and the steady decline in numbers of this people. No intelligent man who has lived on the frontier for the last quarter of a century can but be impressed with the utter impracticability of these contending factions ever living together in peace. The efforts of their principal men, by the treaty of 1846, to allay the deadly strife, proved utterly futile. Murder and assassination followed upon its heel, and showed that the implacable spirit engendered by the treaty of 1835 was inground in the people, and that no efforts of their chiefs could allay it. The reports of every superintendent, agent, and commissioner upon the Cherokee people, now on file in your office, demonstrate this.

You invite me " to make any suggestions which may be of service to the government in arranging the difficulties between them," (the factions.)

This is a problem which the policy of the government in the past has wholly failed to solve. If the object of the government be to fulfil in the spirit the various treaty stipulations—insure them peace and domestic tranquillity, to enlighten and advance them in the career of civilization, and to make them valuable neighbors and good friends—it is my deliberate opinion, based on an intimate knowledge of this people for a quarter of a century, and which is confirmed by every record in your office bearing upon the subject, that there is but one way to attain it, and that one way is the partition of the Cherokee domain in the proportion of numbers, and the separation of this people into two distinct and separate communities. The necessity of this course of policy has been apparent to the government in the past, and as far back as 1846 President Polk, by a special message, urged it upon the attention of Congress, and advised separation, which recommendation was unheeded, and the treaty of 1846 was entered into, which it was hoped would bring peace to this distracted people. But it was a hollow truce, and the evils it was intended to cure still remain unabated, acquiring strength with time, and which, if not arrested by the only remedy—separation—will result in the destruction of those to whom the government is peculiarly bound to afford protection and relief. This policy brought peace to the distracted parties of the Choctaw Nation. They now form two peoples, Choctaws and Chickasaws, who, ever since the separation, have lived side by side in peace and friendship. So also of the Creeks and Seminoles. The ears of the government have been assailed from year to year with the recital of the brutal assassinations and butcherly murders which have occurred among these hostile factions on the borders of Arkansas, sometimes transgressing the line, exciting the apprehension of the whites, and leading to the organization of military companies. Like causes exist, and like results may be looked for in the future. The question has but one solution—separation.

The feuds among the Cherokees date far back, and have never ceased. The complications in which they were involved by reason of the rebellion only intensified the bitter hatred which already existed, nothing more.

The Cherokee troubles, I submit, should be dealt with practically, regard being had to past facts and future probabilities. The factions, after repeated trials, cannot settle or harmonize; they cannot agree to stop disagreement long enough to effect a plan of adjustment. The government, as umpire and guardian, should therefore do it for them. If the present policy be adhered to, and the government compel these factions to live together, refuse to place political and geographical barriers between them, a repetition of their past broils, feuds, and murders may be looked for, and the continued disquietude of the citizens of the borders of the neighboring States.

Separation of the factions is the only salvation of the Cherokees; the only way by which peace and harmony can be restored to them.

I have only further to say, that in making the above statements and in giving the above opinions I am only moved by a desire to see these people prosperous and happy. I have no interest otherwise in the matter, except so far as their condition affecting Arkansas might be taken as such. I have been treated with courtesy and hospitality by all parties among them, and I sincerely desire to see them harmonious and united.

Before concluding, I wish to submit a few suggestions in reference to the civilized Indian nations west of Arkansas. The cordon of States is drawing closer and closer around them. In my own time, since living on the border, have two States arisen—one on the north, one on the south—and population is rapidly increasing in them all. A repetition of the history of the relations of the eastern Cherokees with the State of Georgia threatens. In a conflict arising between a sovereign State and the anomalous and dependent governmental organizations of the Indian tribes, little forecast is required to determine the result. History will but repeat itself. Is there no remedy? or must these Indian nations fade away before the advancing line of new States and white civilization?

I submit, Mr. Commissioner, that if these different nations were aggregated together under one territorial government with the proper checks and safeguards; if their lands were surveyed and assigned in severalty; if the government would cut the leading strings and let them go, throw them upon their own efforts and resources, to sink or swim, then these people will move forward in civilization, maintain their identity, and win an honorable page in the history of states and nations. Treat them with the utmost liberality in their present unfortunate condition, but pay them the last payment and the last dollar; banish the miserable, corrupting, degrading system of bounties and Indian agencies, and let them go. Then holding their lands in severalty, and relying upon their own energies, their ambition will receive a new, powerful, and hitherto unknown stimulus, and all the great capabilities of the Indian will be developed.

The territorial bill, introduced in the Senate during the last

Congress by Mr. Secretary Harlan, while a member of that body, looks to these ends. It is a measure conceived in the humane spirit of enlightened statesmanship, and, in my judgment, is the only one which will secure to the Indian identity of race, a State civilization, and a history worthy of preservation. I learn that a similar bill is now before Congress, and I trust it may soon become a law.'

Respectfully, your obedient servant,

J. M. TEBBETTS.

Hon. D. N. Cooley,
　　Commissioner Indian Affairs, Washington, D. C.

K.

Letter of Charles B. Johnson to Commissioner of Indian Affairs.

WASHINGTON, D. C.. *May* 7, 1866.

SIR: Yours of the 5th instant came duly to hand. In answer to your inquiries, I will say that the Cherokees are about equally divided as to numbers, "northern and southern." Most of the southern Cherokees have returned to that portion of their country known as the Canadian district, south of the Arkansas. It has not come to my knowledge of any troubles or difficulties between the two parties since the termination of the war, but do not believe it possible for them to live peaceably under the same local government. From my own knowledge, (which has been the experience of twenty-seven years,) the bad feelings existing between the "Ross" and "Watie" parties can never be reconciled.

The worst state of things existed before the war. Since peace has come no change of feeling has taken place. I have been in frequent communication with both parties since the war.

Yours with respect,

CHARLES B. JOHNSON.

Hon. D. N. Cooley,
　　Commissioner of Indian Affairs, Washington, D. C.

L.

Letter of Hon. R. T. Van Horn to Commissioner of Indian Affairs.

HOUSE OF REPRESENTATIVES,
Washington. D. C.., May 10, 1866.

SIR : Your letter of May 5 was received yesterday, making certain inquiries touching the Cherokee Nation of Indians.

I have no means at hand to answer your interrogatory as to population, &c.

I have lived in the west many years, and have had opportunities of forming an opinion in regard to the state of feeling between the two parties in the Cherokee Nation, known as the "Ross party," and "Ridge party," now designated as the "loyal" and "disloyal," respectively.

Ever since their removal from Georgia to the southwest, these parties have been engaged in strife, and I do not believe they will ever be able to remain at peace if united. Blood has been freely shed heretofore, and will continue to be shed as long as one party has control over the other.

If the country had been divided twenty years ago, and the tribe separated, it would have been for the benefit of all; and I have no doubt that any attempt to keep them together in the future will only result in injury to both.

The feud is too old and too bitter ever to be healed.

Truly yours,

R. T. VAN HORN.

Hon. D. N. Cooley,
Commissioner of Indian Affairs.

M.

Letter of General Blunt to Commissioner of Indian Affairs.

WASHINGTON, D. C., *May 4, 1866.*

SIR: In answer to your letter of yesterday, asking my views relative to the condition of the Cherokee Indians, northern and southern, their numbers, location, &c., and the probability of their reuniting and living together as one people, I have the honor to state that during the greater part of the time from May, 1862, to the close of the war, the southwestern Indian country was embraced within my command. The three regiments of loyal Indians were organized under my supervision, and served with me in the field in Arkansas and the Indian territory, in the campaigns of 1862 and 1863. And during the fall of 1865, since the termination of the war, I spent considerable time in the Cherokee Nation.

During all this time my relation with the Cherokee country was such as to afford me opportunities of becoming intimately acquainted with the status or condition of the Cherokee people, and to ascertain the relations existing between what is known as the loyal and disloyal portions of the tribe or nation.

In the fall of 1865, when I was last in the Cherokee Nation, the number of southern or disloyal Cherokees was between six thousand and seven thousand, which number comprised less than one-half of the entire aggregate of the Cherokee people. They were then located north of Red river, in the Choctaw and Chickasaw country, while the loyal Cherokees were occupying their former homes in their own country. What portion of the southern Cherokees, or whether any have since returned to their homes in the Cherokee country, I am unable to answer, as I have no information on the subject.

As to the "probability of the two parties of Cherokees, northern and southern, reuniting, and living together as one people," I am clearly of the opinion that such a policy is impracticable, and would be inimical to the interests of both parties, and that the peace and security of each require their separation.

The reasons upon which I base this opinion are briefly these : It is well known that for many years prior to the late war a bitter feud existed between two factions of the Cherokee people. One of these factions now comprises the loyal Cherokees, and the other comprises the southern or disloyal Cherokees, and during the last four or five years this feud has become greatly intensified by the events of the war ; and from my knowledge of the bitter hostility they manifest towards each other and of the peculiar traits of Indian character, I do not think it probable that amicable relations can again be restored among them, so as to admit of their living together in peace and harmony as one people under the same local jurisdiction. I believe that however much the leading men of both factions may exert themselves to preserve peace and security to life and property, their efforts will prove futile, unless they are separated and each party have their own municipal regulations. If this should not be done, and both factions are compelled to unite as one people, and be subject to such laws and regulations as may be prescribed by the dominant party, then the bitter party feuds, resulting in assassination and bloodshed that was so common prior to the war, will now be increased ten-fold; and in the execution of the local laws little protection will be afforded to those who may be the victims of persecution by members of the dominant party.

Without expressing any opinion as to the manner of their separation, or as to the section of country that should be set apart for the location of each party, I am quite confident that the mutual welfare of both factions of the Cherokees demands that they should be separated and located in different portions of their territory, where neither party shall be subject to the local laws and regulations of the other.

I have the honor to be, very respectfully, your obedient servant,
JAS. G. BLUNT,
Late Major General.

Hon. D. N. COOLEY,
   Commissioner of Indian Affairs.

N.

Letter of D. H. Cooper to Commissioner of Indian Affairs.

WASHINGTON, *May* 16, 1866.

SIR : Having learned that it is your desire that I should furnish the Indian Office with any information in my possession relative to the present condition of the Cherokee Indians, both northern and southern, their location, numbers, &c., &c., especially as regards the probability of their reuniting and living together as one people, together with my views and any suggestions which may be of service to the government in arranging the difficulties between them, in compliance therewith I have the honor to state. that for a number of years past I have had but little accurate information of the condition and numbers of the northern Cherokees. Before the late war they were located principally north of the Arkansas river, east of Grand river, south of the Spavinaw, a tributary of Grand river, and west of the State line of Arkansas.

The southern Cherokees, before they left the Cherokee Nation, re-sided, mostly, west of Grand river, on the Verdigris and its branches, and in what is known as the Canadian district, in the forks of the Arkansas and Canadian rivers, and east of the Creek country. There were many exceptions to this classification, some of each party having resided within the localities inhabited mainly by the members of the opposite party. The present condition of the southern Cherokees is one of extreme poverty and destitution. A few of them have returned to the Cherokee country north of the Arkansas river; many are located in the Canadian district, and not a few yet remain among the Choctaws and Chickasaws. There are also many in Texas and other States, exiles from their country.

At the date of the surrender of the army of the Confederate States in the trans-Mississippi department, the number of southern Cherokees was estimated, by those having the best means of accurate information on the subject. at five thousand five hundred. It would be safe, I think, to set down the southern Cherokees at something between six and seven thousand souls.

I have no means of arriving at the numbers and condition of the northern Cherokees, except the statistics embraced in the document accompanying your annual report for the year 1865.

At one time during the late war between the United States and the so-called Confederate States, the troops raised by the two opposing parties (the Ross and the Watie) among the Cherokees, for the service of the latter, were under my command, and I had frequent ample opportunity to observe the temper of these parties towards each other. I found an irreconcilable feud and the most deadly hostility existing between them, which I in vain attempted to remove; and I am entirely satisfied the members of the present generation among them will never live at peace together under the same government, unless forced to do so by military authority.

And knowing the characteristic tendency of the Indian race to nurse and keep alive their feuds, and to transmit the desire for revenge to their posterity, I doubt very much whether the deadly hate now existing between the Ross and Watie parties will be eradicated in another generation.

Entertaining this belief, I do not hesitate to give my opinion—and I do it without the slightest prejudice or ill-feeling—that it is not only the true interest of these two parties among the Cherokees that they should be separated and located in distinct districts, with independent legislatures, but that it is the duty of the United States government to require this to be done, as the very best means of protecting them against "domestic strife."

It is true the United States can, by keeping up a large standing military force among them, and by assuming the reins of government in the Cherokee Nation, reduce these people to subjection, and compel them to respect each other's rights; but this, it is apparent, would involve very heavy expense, and the violation of existing treaties, by depriving the whole Cherokee people, northern and southern, of the right of self-government.

Of the alternatives it seems to me a separation of the discordant elements would be the most desirable and most acceptable to all parties.

In this connexion I would most respectfully suggest, inasmuch as the two parties have a common interest in the Cherokee country and in the Cherokee funds, that an equitable division be made and a district or districts assigned to each, with well-defined boundaries, and that each party have guaranteed to them, by the United States, the right of jurisdiction and self-government over and within their respective limits; giving to the members of both parties the right freely to settle within the jurisdiction of the other, with all the rights, privileges, and immunities of citizens thereof, inclusive of the right to vote and hold office.

To adopt this plan would not be experimental. There is a precedent under the tripartite treaty of June, 1855, between the United States, the Choctaws, and the Chickasaws.

It has succeeded admirably with the Choctaws and Chickasaws, who, before the conclusion of that treaty, were rapidly becoming hostile to each other, and, but for the wise and timely settlement of their difficulties by the United States in 1855, doubtless bloodshed would have resulted.

I am, very respectfully, your obedient servant,

DOUGLAS H. COOPER.

Hon. D. N. Cooley,
Commissioner of Indian Affairs,
Department of the Interior, Washington City.

O.

Letter of J. B. Luce to Commissioner of Indian Affairs.

Washington, May 25, 1866.

Sir: In reply to your inquiries as to the present condition of the northern and southern Cherokees, and the probability of their reuniting and living together again as one people, I have to state that my information relates rather to the past than to the present.

I first became acquainted with Cherokee affairs while a clerk in the Indian Office, from February, 1838, to April, 1841. It was part of my duty to read and register all the letters received during the disturbances of 1839. I was afterwards clerk to the southern superintendent, the late Major William Armstrong, who took a leading part in making the treaty of 1846, and with whom I was then living. Up to that time, so far as my information extended, the opinion prevailed very generally that the feuds between the contending parties were irreconcilable, and that they could not live together in peace under one tribal government. The accounts which Major Armstrong gave of the efforts made by the leaders of the different parties on that occasion to effect a cordial reconciliation were such as to induce the belief that the trial was then made under the most favorable circumstances, and for a while it seemed that the pacification was likely to be permanent. In 1848 my connexion with the Indian department terminated. Since then my opportunities for obtaining a knowledge of Cherokee affairs have been such only as were common to other citizens of Arkansas living near the Indian line. From time to time I have heard of the killing of prominent Cherokees identified with the parties at strife before 1846, but do not know enough of the circumstances to say how far they were connected with political causes. In 1861 there were decided indications that the old animosity between the Ross and Ridge parties still existed, and that in some quarters it was as strong as ever. In 1862 other circumstances tended to confirm this impression. Since 1862 I have had no means of knowing anything of Cherokee affairs except from southern Cherokees now in this city.

It will thus be seen that my information on the subject of your inquiries relates more especially to the treaty of 1846 and the seven or eight preceding years. I have always believed that whatever may have occurred before its date, that treaty was the expression of an honest, well-meant effort of the leaders on all sides to restore peace and harmony. If that effort failed, it seems to me but little could be hoped from any other. Any attempt to secure a reunion without the cordial concurrence and co-operation of the influential men of both parties would, in my opinion, be actually less likely to effect a reconciliation than a formal division or separation. Two instances somewhat analogous occur to me which support this view of the case.

The Chickasaws were left by their treaty of 1832 without a country. Major Armstrong—the same officer to whom I have already referred—made an arrangement or "convention," in 1837, for their admission into the Choctaw country on terms which he thought favorable to them, but which they were induced to accept only because they could in no other way secure a home. The two tribes speak substantially the same language. There had never been any feuds or hostilities to separate them. There was nothing that any outsider could perceive to prevent their becoming one people. Yet the objections, to all appearance imaginary, of the Chickasaw minority, equal to about one-fourth of the combined tribes, produced a running sore, which, in 1855, threatened serious mischief; so much so that the convention of 1837, after eighteen years' trial, was abrogated, and the separate government of the Chickasaws restored. During the ten years of separation the tendency to union has been

5

increasing, and the two tribes are actually bound together more closely at this moment than at any time while nominally united under a treaty.

In 1845 the same officer, Major Armstrong, as president of a board of commissioners to negotiate a treaty with the Creeks and Seminoles, effected an arrangement for the latter tribe under similar circumstances, and similar in its character to that made for the Chickasaws in 1837, the same degree of reluctance on the part of the homeless minority being shown in both cases. There was in fact a striking parallelism all the way through—the same apparent natural causes for union—the causes for disunion apparently trivial and imaginary—the real difficulty in both cases arising from the want of consent on the part of the smaller tribe. The union of the Choctaws and Chickasaws lasted eighteen years; that of the Creeks and Seminoles eleven. The latter was abrogated in 1856, and, as in the other case, was followed by a stronger tendency to consolidation than had previously existed.

As already remarked, I am for these reasons led to doubt that the reunion of the Cherokees can be effected so long as it is resisted by any considerable portion of either one of the contending parties.

Very respectfully, your most obedient servant,

J. B. LUCE.

Hon. D. N. COOLEY,
  Commissioner of Indian Affairs.

www.ingramcontent.com/pod-product-compliance
Lightning Source LLC
Chambersburg PA
CBHW021637270326
41931CB00008B/1063